Jackie Rear

Hans Dekk

MINDSET
FOR
FOOTBALL

A mental revolution
for teenagers to professionals
A proven method used by Olympic athletes

FOREWORD BY
SARINA WIEGMAN

MINDSET PUBLISHERS

to Willy Dullens

This book is published by
Mindset Publishers
IJsbaanpad 43
1076 CV Amsterdam
www.friendlyeyes.com

Graphic design: Aart Jan Bergshoeff
Graphic modifications from 2018 - Robert Koopman – www.warmgrijs.nl
Cover designed by: Lalita Poole, www.maxidesignstudio.com

ISBN 978 90 827974 3 5
NUR 482

Photocredits: Punch/acceptance © Tetra Images/Corbis
Good Mistakes: © Fotolia
Eagle: © Dreamstime

CONTENT

FOREWORD
BY
SARINA WIEGMAN

Over the past few years, I have met Jackie on numerous occasions. She led a workshop that I attended and we also met up during Topsport Community activities in the Netherlands, initiated by Pieter van den Hoogenband (*ex-Olympic swimmer, 3 gold medals and Chef de Mission of the Dutch Olympic athletes*), where science, sport, and the corporate and music world exchange their knowledge with one another. One second, we were chatting; the next moment, at a workshop given by former World Champion professional boxer Lucia Rijker, we were boxing with each other! We clicked immediately and it was clear to me from the start how energetic and inspiring Jackie is.

As a football coach, I find it fantastic to see how passionate the players I work with are, real lovers of this beautiful sport. I consider taking good care of players and staff one of a coach's most important tasks. To see the player as a human being—not just a football player—and to help her develop, on and off the field. It's also essential to treat all teammates with respect, to be open and positively critical. We have a common goal: to perform at the top of our game and at the same time to have and keep having as much fun as possible in what we do.

I think it is important to involve not only the players but also the staff in the team process. To reach the highest level, we need to be clear and open with each other, to be short and to the point. It is up to me to create that safe environment where everyone feels seen and dares to speak out.

In the book *Mindset for Football*, you will learn how to avoid getting bogged down in 'Story Thinking' and also how important it is to realise when you are judging. When too many thoughts start to 'haunt' your mind, you become distracted from the things that are (more) important. This book helps you to focus on the things that do matter, without being distracted. This mindset is called 'Action Thinking'.

What I particularly like is that you learn to understand how to deal with pressure in a practical way and consciously choose Action Thinking (rather than Story Thinking).

Another aspect that appeals to me in the *Mindset* approach is the expression 'Friendly Eyes'. This means, among other things, learning to observe yourself and others without judgment. People, and therefore athletes too, tend to blame teammates, the referee or any other external factor when things go wrong. That doesn't help you to concentrate, it doesn't improve the game and it also gets in the way of your own development.

For these reasons, it's my pleasure to contribute as an ambassador for Jackie's *Friendly Eyes* movement. *Friendly Eyes* is an online mental training programme in which you learn to be (more) resilient, with kindness as the starting point. This way of coaching suits me.

I hope that this book will also inspire you and show you how you can create a safe environment in which you can make mental progress.

Happy reading and learning ... and especially, Friendly Eyes!

Sarina Wiegman

SARINA WIEGMAN'S ADVICE

HOW CAN YOU GET THE MOST OUT OF THIS BOOK?

To help you as a reader see how you too can make this mental progress and get the most out of this book, I would like to add the following:

According to *Mindset*, technical improvement can best be achieved by focusing on 'feeling instead of thought'. In the world of football, you can see this as improving a football skill. And these skills could be improved by training based on implicit learning. It's about the unconscious and automatic learning of skills. Players concentrate on improving their technique without being hindered by constantly thinking about their technique and instead focus on the football action, for example a pass at the right moment, in the right direction and with the right speed to bring a teammate into a scoring position.

Football is played in a context in which players have to deal with fellow players, opponents, the playing field (space and time) and the rules of the game. In football training, you try to keep this context in mind. It is always about making the right choices and performing the right actions in attack, defence and conversion. The technique (e.g., passing or controlling the ball) is a tool for doing this.

You will get the most out of this book if you read it with this information about technique in mind.

A MENTAL REVOLUTION FOR TEENAGERS TO PROFESSIONALS

Our book is about the mental side of football, which is finally becoming recognised as an important part of every player's journey.

The traditional mindset of bullying players into giving their best effort and demanding that they keep silent about any challenging issues they might be experiencing, is still unfortunately present. However, it is clear that a revolution is taking place when it comes to the importance of mental wellbeing. We invite you to be part of that revolution.

We are very grateful and honoured that Sarina Wiegman has written the foreword to our book, where she emphasises the crucial importance of the mental side in football.

Mindset for Football is based on universal principles. It is not merely a mental guide for football, but also an awareness guide, using **football** as a metaphor to realise how unconscious so much of our behaviour is.

***Mindset* works in 4 stages:**

1. Making a conscious choice to adopt Action Thinking instead of Story Thinking.
2. Six pillars for more self-knowledge and better self-management.
3. Four types of concentration for attention control.
4. The Instruments for achieving mental tranquility.

It was my pleasure to train upcoming teenage football players in the Netherlands for ten years. The Dutch education system allowed the young players to combine school with football. All of the exercises described in this book were used to motivate and guide the teenagers to stay focused and learn how to enjoy challenges on and off the pitch. These players I believe to be true pioneers, as when we started, there were very few opportunities for female players. They chose to believe in themselves and due to their courage and that of their coaches, they have created a path for many to follow. Most of them are now playing professionally and loving the game, some of them play for the Dutch National team and competed at the Olympic games.

Our philosophy is based on the belief that we have a choice as to how to approach the world and ourselves. We describe a course of life that you may decide to adopt.

A great example of this philosophy came to life in the summer of 2022. In a full Wembley Stadium, the Lionesses, under the inspirational guidance of Sarina Wiegman, heroically beat Germany 2-1 in the European Cup final in extra time.

The way I see it Sarina had set out a clear plan for the team and all staff members that was based on transparency, trust and team values, combined with the true belief that winning every match was possible. These values constantly prevailed above all external expectations and pressures. According to Leah Williamson in an interview with Sky Sports, Sarina said calmly to the team before the final: '*We don't need to win today, we just really, really want to. Go out there, do your very best and enjoy it*'. This way of communicating to the players is, as I see it, not only clear and powerful, but also compassionate and kind. Leah went on to say; '*Sarina's changed things in terms of how we didn't chase the end goal, we chased the day-to-day, which does make a difference. When you make it habitual and you get up every day and just do your job, you know exactly what you're there for and you just tick little boxes off and when you get to these games, it's just another step on the journey, which she made a reality for us but also the belief that we were going to do something good.*'

By addressing the players like this, I believe that Sarina helped them understand that when they are busy with pressure they are not occupied with the job. She spoke calmly with them at all times, no shouting or swearing, just a clear message again and again, explaining what she wanted the team to focus on. She created a culture and environment where everyone felt safe, could excel and be genuinely happy.

Readers, it's now time for you to revolutionise your mindset! Making the choice to become an Action Thinker is possible for anyone who is willing to make the effort. This book and the online courses will teach you how to do that in a practical way. Friendly Eyes is the first pillar of Action Thinking, and is the key to achieving a balanced mind. If you look with Friendly Eyes, objectively and non-judgmentally – at yourself and the world around you – emotions will lose their power over you.

#friendlyeyes Jackie Reardon

ONLINE MENTAL TRAINING

The video concentration course 'Discover' shows you how to apply *Mindset* practically both on and off the football pitch.

There are many films showing practical exercises used by teenage football players who eventually became well known professional players. The exercises are easy to understand and fun to do at any level.

The learnings seamlessly connect to this book and are presented by Jackie Reardon.

WWW.FRIENDLYEYES.COM/DISCOVER

MINDSET AS AN ADVENTURE

THE WHY

This book will guide you, one step at a time, towards a better mindset. A 'mindset' is a way of thinking. A mentally strong player has a particular way of thinking, which we call 'Action Thinking'. We refer to the opposite way of thinking as 'Story Thinking'. This book explains how Story Thinking can be changed into Action Thinking. By choosing for Action Thinking you will be embarking on an exciting and unparalleled adventure, one that can bring about lasting change.

Everyone is familiar with the constant noise of distracting thoughts that interfere with everything we're doing and what we really want to be concentrating on. Sometimes it seems as if our heads are full of doubts, insecurities, and frustrations. It is like the constant buzz of mosquitoes that stops us achieving the sensation that we call 'flow' or 'being in the zone'. And we all want to be in the zone in everything we do. Whether it's playing football, making a deadline, acting effectively at a meeting, or making music. We'd like to be able to keep those mosquitoes at bay, as much as possible. The constant noise of thoughts in the background we call 'Story Thinking', and we set out here to explain how to convert 'Story Thinking' into 'Action Thinking'. We will teach you how to convert your mind with its endless noise and running commentary into a state of rest, balance, and awareness.

More and more players now realise the overriding importance of the mental side of football, and know that you can improve your game immensely by working on it. Dwelling too long on your own mistakes or the mistakes made by others in the team, focusing too much on the score, fighting yourself and maybe even your teammates: everyone knows that these things happen during matches, causing you to tense up and make unnecessary mistakes. This attitude also takes away your enjoyment of the game.

Of course having good technical skills is an indispensable part of the game at every level, but our emphasis here is on the mental side of football.

The understanding you can gain here can certainly be used while you are working on improving your football skills: you can learn to make the improvements you want in an enjoyable way. You do this by changing the habit patterns of your mind.

We shall give you tools that will help you to set about improving and strengthening your mental powers. The key is to invest instead of to consume. The most important investment you can make, both for yourself and for your team, is to set clear mental goals. In Chapter 9, you will learn how to set your goals. When you do this in combination with online concentration course *Discover* you will get the best results. There are many videos with exercises that explain in pictures what we explain here in words.

Mindset for Football will teach you how to conquer your fears and to calm your thoughts, using Action Thinking. Under the pressure of a match (or in the stress of everyday life) you may often find that you lose the sense of ease with which you perform to the best of your ability. Every player will recognise the feeling of 'the last minutes of the match': suddenly your heart starts beating faster, tension rushes through your body, all you can think about is: 'if only we keep our lead' or 'if only we score' or 'if only we stay level' or 'I can't believe we are going to lose this match' or 'if only they don't score'. We are going to teach you how to turn these energy-consuming thoughts and feelings into a powerful end of the match, full of energy.

Deploying the right *Instruments* will evoke Action Thinking, we will explain all of the *Instruments* later. During the match itself, scanning and zooming (visual concentration) take over, and thoughts become short and clear by implementing the Instruments. We shall be basing ourselves here on the work of Dr. Robert Nideffer (attention control studies), to clarify this process and scientific studies showing exactly how top athletes use their eyes during matches. In our view, all thoughts should be disengaged once the action in the match has begun. Decisions should be taken instinctively. This may sound exaggerated or even peculiar, but if we listen to what leading sports personalities say about a 'flow', it always comes down to the same thing: 'I didn't think, I acted.' *Mindset* enhances instinct.

Mindset has developed a vocabulary that is concrete, simple, modern and accessible. It is 'accessible' in the sense that the terminology is neutral/objective rather than confrontational. Take this example. When a coach asks a player or the team: 'Is there any Story Thinking going on?', it will have a very different impact than when they ask: 'Why are you so tensed up?' We have seen the impact of this in training sessions and this makes a world of difference. In fact we constantly hear that teammates tell each other that they were 'in Story Thinking', without any of the depressing, frustrating overtones that usually accompany such situations. In other words, this terminology tends to motivate people instead of making them feel hurt or put down and creates the necessary distance to observe your mental state instead of losing yourself. And since the vocabulary is simple and even slightly amusing sometimes, it soon becomes clear where the work has to be done. It also gives the player more insight into her or his own responsibility. Better self-management gives people the energy they need to make changes.

Mindset provides coaches with a general framework for communicating with their team, using one or two words instead of complex sentences. This makes it possible to communicate about the mental side of the game in a specific, simple and tangible manner. Coaches often use an awful lot of words, sometimes even screaming at the players out of pure frustration, which has the unintentional effect of 'helping' their team stay in Story Thinking. In this book, our philosophy is applied to football. But the two mindsets can be applied to any activity, using football as a metaphor.

Consider, for a moment, the different ways in which someone may make music. The Story Thinker plays notes. Technically, everything may be perfect, but there is not the slightest bit of feeling in the way she plays. Her mind is filled with too many thoughts that are buzzing noisily in the background, as mosquitoes do. The Action Thinker interprets. For her, the notes are just a basis to go on. 'That was played with great feeling' is a comment that has nothing to do with Story Thinking and everything to do with Action Thinking. The same applies to communication. Sometimes you may fill in all the gaps yourself when someone is trying to tell you something. What you hear fits precisely into the image that you already had of the person. This is the Story Thinker's judgment. It may turn out to be very surprising if you listen actively, with more empathy and try, without making any judgment, to understand the real motives behind the person's words. You may suddenly realise that you've never listened properly to them before, with an Action Thinker's attention, but were already thinking up your own story or answer while they were still speaking. In other words, you were stuck in the thoughts of Story Thinking instead of the feeling of Action Thinking.

The inspiration for this book was drawn from Jackie's 10 years experience coaching semi-professional female football players, her guidance of many Olympic teams and also as a coach leading over a hundred tennis holidays from 1991 'til 2014. Over the past years Jackie has guided captains of industries from multiple disciplines; from the business world to the sports field, and from Opera houses to the professional tennis world. The insight meditation training of S.N. Goenka ('*Vipassana*') www.dhamma.org, was life changing for Jackie and set the course for all of the *Mindset* books and the Friendly Eyes online platform.

For those of you who are interested in books that present scientific insights which are very much in line with our method, we recommend the following books: *The Talent Code* by Daniel Coyle, *My Stroke of Insight* by Jill Bolte Taylor, *Mindset* by Carol Dweck and *Breaking the habit of being yourself* by Joe Dispenza.

It is with joy and humbleness that we can truly state, that everyone who adopts an open mind to our approach will benefit from it and become a more complete human being.

MINDSET IN A NUTSHELL

OUR PHILOSOPHY

All around us, there are signs of a movement away from the lifestyle and way of thinking that are associated with the rat race towards a more conscious way of living and thinking. Mindfulness, slowing down the pace of life and stress management are all terms that no longer sound vague or esoteric. We call the traditional mentality of judging, rationalising and attachment to the past and the future 'Story Thinking'. The new way of thinking that *Mindset for Football* advocates is governed by observing non-judgmentally and focusing on the here and now by giving quality to everything you do. We call this balanced mindset 'Action Thinking'.

By changing your mindset, you will get the best out of yourself, and you will find yourself able to do far more than before with the same level of skill. Getting into a flow is within anyone's reach, provided you know what to focus on. *Mindset for Football* is a mental guide that teaches you to change from Story Thinking into Action Thinking. You will learn how to be in the here and now, and to conquer the interference coming from the ego. Winning from yourself will become more important than beating the other team. Once you have mastered this way of thinking, you will always be able to give your best performance.

Someone who could often serve as a good role model is Lionel Messi. He literally says he plays football because he loves it and because he wants to constantly improve himself. He says he does not want to compare himself to anyone else but strives only to improve his previous performance. His success comes from a constant drive to perform at a higher level. He has learned to improve his concentration to a level at which his achievements are derived almost entirely from Action Thinking. We saw Messi in the ultimate action thinking state, during the World Cup final in 2022, where Argentina beat France in a breathtaking penalty-shoot out. Messi took two penalties in that match, one at the 23rd minute and one in the final penalty shoot-out. He managed to close himself off from all external pressure and focus on the here and now. The calmness in which he successfully converted the two penalties was clear for all to see. The first goal he placed perfectly in the right lower corner, the second goal in the left lower corner. What clarity of mind. Of course, it's impossible to teach you to play like Messi - that is total madness! But what we do believe we can teach you, is to how to achieve a mental state of calmness under pressure. This will only happen if a player is open to change.

In general we tend to resist change, because our usual patterns feel comfortable; changing patterns requires energy and effort, and is sometimes confrontational and painful. We are always searching for excuses to avoid change. The only way of changing old patterns into new ones is through practice and repetition. Every day you practise means progress. This is an essential element of the *Mindset* philosophy. Shifting from story to Action Thinking does not mean that we have to turn our thoughts off altogether, it means finding new patterns to help us neutralise the 'noise' of Story Thinking and not to identify with it. We have a choice. That's the only way we can learn to perfect our focus. This book pays little attention to technique or strategy, but strangely enough, everyone who reads *Mindset for Football* will nonetheless find that they make progress in these two areas. That is because mental factors influence and control everything you do.

In Story Thinking, there is a big difference between winning and losing; the result is quite obviously the deciding factor. Action Thinking makes it possible to win every time. If you are bogged down in Story Thinking, you and your team have simply won or lost, in football terms, according to the score. In Action Thinking you can win twice: from yourself, and in addition, sometimes from the other team. You win from yourself if you set realistic goals for yourself and your team beforehand, in a match as well as in a training session, and achieve them by carrying out your plan consistently and with discipline. You will learn to experience this as a victory. Eventually you will start to realise that winning from yourself is more important than winning from the other team. Wanting to win remains exceptionally important, but it is not the be all and end all of your life. And with this attitude will come a new feeling of self-confidence.

'My only goal is to win this match.' This is something you will hear football players of all levels say more frequently than almost anything else. And the funny thing about this statement is that it essentially has no content at all. This winning does not serve any goal, no specific plan has been mapped out that can be worked on, it does not provide any guidelines as to what you hope to achieve, and all it does is add tension. Bettine Vriesekoop (twice European table-tennis champion) wrote the following comment in response to the first edition of *Mindset*: 'If you think in terms of winning or losing you're always in a position of dependency. If you give quality to all your actions, the results will come by themselves.'

Mindset for Football is not about learning a few useful tips, although there will be a few of those along the way. It is about something much more important. It is about changing our whole way of thinking about football and about ourselves.

FEELING (USE THE INSTRUMENTS)

The magic that will enable you to discard Story Thinking and shift to Action Thinking is finding the right 'feeling'. The method explained in *Mindset* will teach you exactly how to find that feeling. You will use one or more of the nine specific Instruments which will help you gain body awareness. Using the Instruments will also enable you to overcome your emotions and to concentrate at the highest level.

One of the most familiar sporting experiences, something that everyone has felt from time to time, is tensing up and choking. You try desperately to remain light-footed, but stay rooted to the spot. A growing sense of confusion sets in; you have no idea what you should do with the ball. Thoughts keep flashing through your mind. These are the mosquitoes attacking you. An Action Thinker learns how to chase the mosquitoes away, he activates himself by using for instance trigger words, breathing techniques, visualisation or rituals. This shifts his focus to the visual, without intervening and paralysing thoughts or emotions.

Above, we mention a few of the Instruments that allow you to navigate from thought to feeling to move into Action Thinking. Everyone will recognise these tools, but very few find them easy to apply or simply forget to use them. People are constantly surprised that negative emotions and thoughts keep getting in the way. And they have no idea what to do about it, what sort of training might be useful.

Finding mental peace and enjoyment is crucial, according to Lionel Messi. He says: "I used to play selfishly, I just wanted to score goals. Now I realise it's not about scoring goals, it's about being in the game, being active with and without the ball, making good decisions and when I'm on the ball, not losing it. By focusing on this, I also have more fun.'

We cannot emphasise enough that 'using the Instruments to gain the right feeling' is a process that cannot be evoked simply by using a few devices on the football field (with Instruments such as visualisation, trigger words, breathing and rituals). The learning process begins outside of the pitch. It is only when you have achieved a change in mindset that the Instruments that can be deployed during a match can be really effective and enable you to shift into Action Thinking. In other words, if you want to achieve Action Thinking during a football match, you have to lay the foundations in everyday life. That is the essence of making your own unique Mindset Goals that is presented for you to use in Chapter 9. There are no quick, short-term solutions although ironically you will notice immediate results. Mental growth is a process of consciousness-raising. The foundations on which you can build this growth are the six pillars, and the four concentration forms.

OUR METHOD - AN OVERVIEW

The aim of *Mindset* is to provide a method that will enable people to develop mental toughness both in matches and in other situations. The method aims at consciousness-raising, with the ultimate aim of acting unconsciously. Eventually you learn to use the Instruments automatically which enables you to have clear thoughts and perfect visual perception.

The basic conditions that are mentioned below are the six pillars that underpin our method. We regard these six pillars as universally applicable. We shall return to all of them many times throughout the book. The *Mindset* Mindmap hereafter will also be clarified throughout the book.

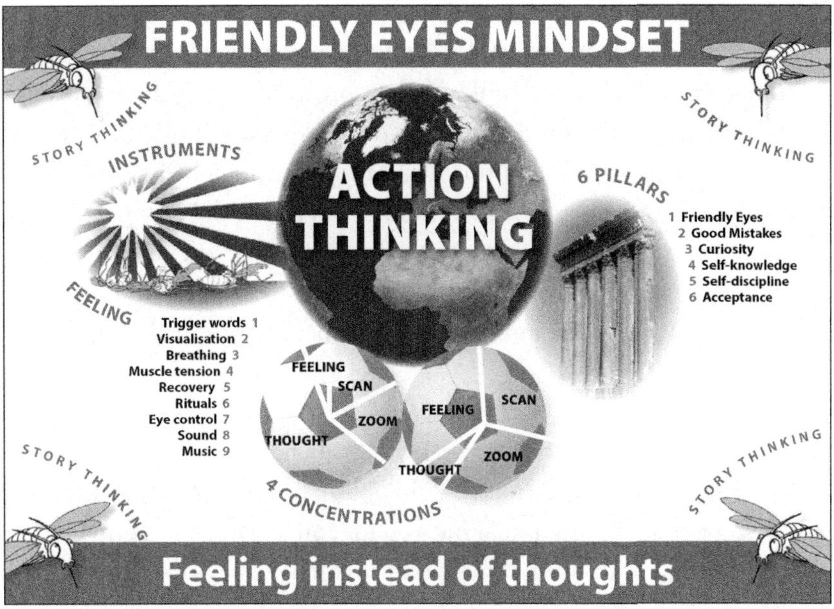

THE SIX PILLARS

1. **Friendly Eyes**
2. **Good Mistakes**
3. **Curiosity**
4. **Self-knowledge**
5. **Self-discipline**
6. **Acceptance**

1. Friendly Eyes

Friendly Eyes and Good Mistakes are the two most important 'pillars' on which to base your development as an Action Thinker. They are the foundation of becoming a mentally resilient and balanced football player. If you look with Friendly Eyes, objectively and non-judgmentally – not just at yourself but also at the world around you – emotions will lose their power over you. This will make you less vulnerable, since you will not take everything personally.

An example of Friendly Eyes in relation to the opposing team: 'If the other team tries to disrupt our game with intimidating comments or behaviour, we shall not get irritated or see it as a personal attack or a way to distract us. We will not let it influence us. In fact we can even understand why they might act that way.' By doing this, you, your team and coach, avoid lapsing into Story Thinking. You protect yourself by adopting a friendly attitude instead. Here is an example of Friendly Eyes in relation to yourself: 'I don't get furious with myself for playing way below my standard, because I understand that I am doing the best I can at this given moment.' By thinking along these lines, you avoid getting stuck in Story Thinking, and allow yourself to quickly return to Action Thinking. 'Friendly Eyes' is a state of mind that every football player should pursue.

2. Good Mistakes

If you boldly pursue a specific goal, you may not succeed straight away. In fact it would be quite odd if you did not make a few mistakes along the way, before you succeed in making a change successful and permanent.

Every player knows how important it is to be able to receive the ball openly. If during this brave, new attempt you lose track of the ball because you did not scan and see the opponent, consider this a good mistake. Or if your attention was too focused on your opponents causing the ball to jump off your foot due to lack of zooming, this is also a good mistake.

Another example: when a football player walks off the pitch totally disillusioned because of a lost match, this person can react in two ways. They learn from what happened, see the match as a 'good mistake'. They realise that progression is not always immediately visible and they continue focusing on personal development with bravery. Or they see their failure as a personal tragedy, closing themselves off to learn from the experience. The latter attitude keeps a football player from making progress and brings a distance between the players and also the coach. 'Good Mistakes' is a way of responding to tangible mistakes, turning every result into a learning process.

3. Curiosity

If you are curious about how you behave on and off the football field, you will gather information to help you enhance your performance. This information may be about your own game, how the other team plays, but also about the emotions that come to the surface. Self-management begins with curiosity, and this includes asking open questions. For example asking an experienced mental coach or psychologist or your team coach: 'What do you think the best way is for me to improve mentally?' The brain can be trained, just like a muscle. So curiosity is very valuable, since it leads to new discoveries that can help you to make changes. Once you realise this, there is no longer any such thing as failure, 'good' and 'bad' become meaningless concepts: there is just scope for growth. Curiosity helps you recognise when you lapse into Story Thinking. The earlier, and the more frequently, you recognise this, the easier it becomes to 'switch' to Action Thinking. The point is that you learn to realise that you have a choice. The consciousness that you have this choice may weigh heavily on you at the beginning, like a big responsibility.

But you could also see it as an exciting discovery. If you view the choice as an exciting adventure, and you don't mind sometimes – or even quite often – 'failing', you will be able to change your mindset far more quickly. In our philosophy, there is in fact no such thing as failure if you do your best. Accept that even when things are 'not working', that doesn't necessarily mean that you're not doing your best. Making mistakes is part of the learning process, and that's why we refer to 'Good Mistakes'. Do not deny the mosquitoes that so often return to you (Story Thinking). Don't be afraid of them, look them straight in the face without judging. Don't identify with them, adopt a certain distance from them and choose Action Thinking by using the tools we provide in this book. These tools will ensure that you feel safe, as a result of which you can conquer your fear. Only when you feel safe you can feel true curiosity. And curiosity leads to self-knowledge.

4. Self-knowledge

Self-knowledge grows through shared knowledge. Self-knowledge does not only come from solitary reflection; more importantly, it comes from asking for open, honest feedback, for instance from your coach, teammates, friends or parents. Self-knowledge will always remain limited if you are not open to the opinions of others. Self-knowledge is an essential part of setting goals, since you need to know what is within your own capabilities. Every player who is involved in football needs to set a mental goal as well as setting goals in technique, tactics and fitness. It is crucial to choose a goal that is specific and achievable. What exactly are you demanding of yourself, why, and how are you going to go about it? From this situation you can really start changing things to your advantage..

5. Self-discipline

Letting go of old patterns creates space for change. Deploying new patterns calls for self-discipline, for which patience is absolutely essential. We all realise this, but how do we muster the energy to remain disciplined when the going gets tough? Reflecting on a daily basis about what you want to change and what your long and short term goals are, will motivate you to carry on. Realising what value this change will bring can make self-discipline a pleasure. We feel the need to emphasise that self-discipline is the only real discipline. A person needs to find the fire from within herself, only then can a real change take place. Friendly Eyes and Good Mistakes can help you achieve this. The fact that you are doing everything that is within your power, gives you the fuel to continue and produces the beginnings of acceptance.

6. Acceptance

Once you are aware of what you need to work on and accept this, there will be more space to focus on your strengths. You can use your energy to focus on the positive instead of fighting the negative. This generates a sense of calm, as a result of which your self-confidence will grow. You will be more appreciative of your efforts, which will diminish frustrations and fears and increase your enjoyment. Your self-respect too will be boosted. This will improve your performance and make you into a more balanced person. Acceptance is the mother of all pillars. Once you have gained an understanding of 'as it is, not as you want it to be', you will experience inner strength, and find you have the energy to go on.

THE FOUR CONCENTRATIONS (ATTENTION CONTROL)

Only once the player has understood the concepts of the six pillars, will they be able to work efficiently on the four concentrations (attention control). Concentration is the most important aspect of all sports, but if this is not combined with a balanced mindset (six pillars) it can never be 'purely' trained as the mind keeps getting in the way of focus. There are four forms of concentration, scan, zoom, feeling and thought. Scanning and zooming are modes of visual concentration *outside* your body. Feeling and thought are modes of internal concentration *within* your body. This will all be clarified in Chapter 5 and 6, where we will introduce the *Instruments* that will help you conjour up the right 'feeling' instead of thoughts. It is enough to say for this moment that a balanced mindset is needed to be able to concentrate. Concentration and a balanced mindset are therefore inseparable. These are the two wings that make a bird fly. If one of them does not work the bird cannot fly.

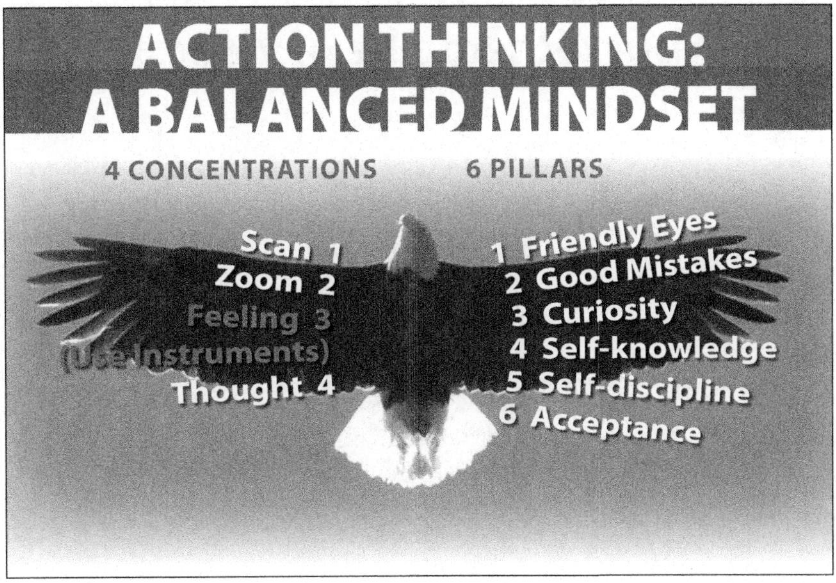

**Strive not to be a success,
but rather to be of value.**

ALBERT EINSTEIN

CHAPTER 1

THE MALFUNCTIONING MACHINE OR PRESENCE OF MIND

CHANGING YOUR MINDSET

This Chapter explains why focus on the mental side of the game always yields the best results provided you make it your number one priority.

Every player would want to achieve the following:

- play freely during matches instead of tensing up.
- be calmly focussed rather than to fight against yourself during a match.
- feel trust and connection rather than irritation with your teammates and coach
- feel confident no matter what team you are playing against
- gain insight into your talents and limitations and that of your teammates.
- know how to turn the fear of failure into confidence and self-assurance.
- know how best to focus/concentrate, both in training and in matches.
- not to be influenced by the score.
- feel acceptance instead of frustration when things aren't going your way.
- to play freely no matter who is watching the match.
- to change the 'battlefield' feeling into a 'playing field' feeling.

In our lives, we are constantly consuming things: food, goods, culture. We do it all the time. All these things change us. And yet we are reluctant to spend time on the most valuable thing in our lives: our mind. Every aspect of our behaviour is determined by our thoughts. Our mindset determines our emotions, and influences our actions and our attitude. Why don't we try to change our mindset, if that will enhance the quality of our lives and improve the way we play football?

Psychological processes are all-important in sport. Driven by the urge to learn, football players will not only improve their football skills, but also gain a better understanding of their actions on and off the football pitch. The reader will go through a plan, in stages, which will set him/her on the path to self-knowledge and a realistic self-image. It would surely give everyone a sense of relief to learn to regard what we call 'failure' – which can have such a devastating effect in our achievement-oriented society – as a totally absurd concept.

Coaches and players of all levels often find themselves facing the same problem. They have spent years working on their technique, tactics and fitness, and it has become clear on both sides (that is, to coaches and players alike) that they have almost reached a certain 'ceiling'. But here is some good news. You can always carry on developing the mental side of your game, and you can even do so when you are not on the football field at all. It will not only provide a new impulse to your game, but it will also give you the motivation that can lead to a more harmonious cooperation between player and coach.

If you don't work on improving, you may lose your self-confidence and your self-respect. Failure exists only if you do nothing. If a certain achievement has eluded us, we may easily regard this as a failure. What we fear most is failure in the eyes of others, more than failure in our own eyes. If we are honest with ourselves, this is what often happens in the field. Everyone can see us failing; that is even more shattering than in everyday life! That is why emotions in football are often almost impossible to control or to understand. Feelings like despair, shame, false pride or agitation may take hold of us. They may paralyse us and make us unsure of ourselves. As soon as we see that we can't fail as long as we set realistic goals and work towards them, our self-confidence will grow and we will enjoy ourselves far more.

If you are having trouble with your game during a match, you can do one of two things: ignore it or work on it. Only in the latter case will you enjoy yourself, although the changes you make may sometimes be difficult. You realise that you have accepted a challenge. That implies growth. Accepting the risk of failure is also growth. Passivity leads to frustration and a loss of self-confidence. Constantly trying to learn, sometimes failing and sometimes succeeding, trying again and again – that will always work much better than doing nothing and waiting to see what happens.

Change your attitude by adopting a new mindset

This book is about changing the way we think about sport and about ourselves. A new mindset, or to use a more philosophical term, a new paradigm. A paradigm is a conceptual framework, a frame of reference, a way of thinking. The most famous paradigm shift is probably the one that Copernicus caused when he stated that the earth rotates around the sun, instead of the other way round. This changed our perceptions not only of the universe, but also of our place as human beings in that universe. The earth was no longer at the centre. Although this book does not deal with revolutionary change on this global scale, within our modest context of the football pitch we are in fact discussing a dramatic change in attitude. As we have explained, it has to do with changing from Story Thinking to Action Thinking. 'Malfunctioning machine' and 'presence of mind' are metaphors we use to clarify this change.

Remember: Story Thinking is characterised by judging yourself and others, focusing (without being aware of it) on the past and the future and rationalising. Action Thinking is observing without judgment, visualising and focusing on the here and now, and giving quality to all your actions.

It is common to find players practising the same technique over and over again, in the solemn belief that 'practice makes perfect'. This repetition is essential, they believe, to attain a higher level. But endlessly repeating the wrong technique is obviously pointless. It will only lead to frustration. In fact, while good practice helps to create good habits, bad practice helps to create bad habits. And frame of mind is an essential part of good practice. To introduce a specific change in technique with precision and finesse required in every facet of football the right kind of concentration.

We cannot emphasise enough that the mental side of your game needs highly regular training in exactly the same way as tactics, technique or fitness. To strengthen a muscle, you have to train it again and again. This process is never 'finished', and the exactly the same applies to training mental processes. If you read this book and then assume that you have now got the hang of this mental stuff, that would be an illusion. Training your mental responses calls for a sustained effort (and relaxation, just as when training muscles!) and is a constant process. But it is also true that a challenging physical workout is just as essential as a challenging mental workout, since you can never change Story Thinking only through mental activity. The mental and physical aspects are inextricably linked. You can only get into Action Thinking by translating mental training into physical activity.

The malfunctioning machine: Story Thinking

At an early age you start playing football with great enthusiasm. On the street with your friends, then off to a club for training. With a lot of dedication you try to learn as much as possible about the game with the images of professional football on TV in the back of your mind. Then, when you start playing real matches, you find that you perform below your expectations. Most coaches and players blame this on the fact that their game skills are not yet at the required level. Although these factors certainly play a role, it is important to note that one's level of play is often much better during training than in matches. Instead of dwelling on this and learning mental lessons from it, both coaches and players often go back to the practice field to train the same drills with the same attitude. Only now, because of the losses, the players must train 'harder and do more'.

Individual players and teams constantly complain about their achievements in matches and express surprise that they almost always play 'below their level' in tournaments and league competition. Within this mindset, technique, physical prowess and strategy are simply Instruments for attaining a single goal: winning matches. In adopting this approach, the players, coaches and parents are unconsciously making themselves a slave of the 'machine' – the machine that is supposed to be providing the right football skills and results. It is not the player but the machine that is responsible. If the machine breaks down, the player and team fail, and also the coach and parents. If and when that happens, all they believe they have to do is then go back to training and continue with the same attitude under the expectation that more training will ensure more winning. Players regularly say after a lost game, 'We just didn't get into the flow of the game. That's how it goes sometimes, pretty unlucky.' The tragedy is that this mindset ensures that the machine never functions optimally and the team, coach and parents, are always dissatisfied.The machine is never good enough.

This process will repeat itself endlessly, at all levels except for the highest professional level and those who have discovered the secret to success: training from Action Thinking. Professional coaches and players know that it involves a process and that it is not just about 'winning and losing'. In this book, you will learn how to train this way.

Presence of mind: Action Thinking

Presence of mind involves a completely different approach. In this way of thinking, football skills are still very important of course, but it is not the beginning and end of the story. The beginning and end of this mindset is self-knowledge.

If players, coaches and parents become conscious of the fact that 'bad' and 'frustrating' play is caused primarily not by problems of technique, tactics or fitness, but by mental factors, they finally start asking themselves the really important question: how can we improve the mental side of our game?

This may all sound rather abstract, and perhaps the reader is thinking: What in heaven's name has all this got to do with football? But by finding out ways in which you can direct your mental responses more efficiently, you will start to experience more energy and enjoyment during your football training and matches.

Those who give up their focus on the 'malfunctioning machine' and switch to an approach based on *presence of mind* will achieve greater satisfaction in their chosen sport and in other areas of life.

Action Thinking and Story Thinking in the spirit of Jung

Every human being has a light side (Action Thinking) and a shadow side (Story Thinking). The famous psychologist Carl Jung called the dark side of the human psyche the Shadow: everything we are but do not want to be. According to Jung, the Shadow is an *unconscious* obstacle that can frustrate even our best intentions. Since it is an unconscious obstacle, it is vital to become familiar with this dark side, in order to deal with it and to modify it into what we do want to be. It is extremely difficult to eliminate the dark side altogether. What we can do, however, is to learn how to deal with it by becoming conscious of it. Exactly the same applies to the way in which we focus our concentration during a match. In football too, it will be a challenge to change our Shadow into a positive experience of the 'Light side'. We first have to become conscious of the Shadow. It is only when we have taken that step (from unconscious incompetence to conscious incompetence) that we can start changing all that negative energy that poisons our concentration into a staged development in the direction of ideal concentration. Even professional players struggle with it in every match. Sometimes people are baffled by the fact that players who have had so much experience and so much coaching still struggle with concentration problems. The answer is easy: the Shadow constantly rears its head. Again and again you find yourself having to do battle with it. Just as you have to practise your technique thousands of times to perfect it, you constantly have to do battle to achieve the right kind of concentration. Don't let this discourage you. It is a challenge. Just as you can eventually learn to execute an excellent long pass by practicing it endlessly, you can also improve your concentration by working at it consistently and diligently.

Who is your toughest opponent?

Your toughest opponent is usually yourself. In matches, you will more often be playing against yourself than against your opponents. Frustration and a sense of powerlessness do not come from your opponents or your teammates, but are caused by yourself. So self-management is crucial. What do you have the power to influence, and what is beyond your influence? With this knowledge, you can become a balanced football player, someone who knows how to train with enjoyment and a sense of well-being. The clearer and more specific your self-management is, the likelier you are to succeed.

Uncertainty is the only certainty you have. In all sports, uncertainty is an essential part of the game. It is learning how to deal with this uncertainty that makes sport so fascinating and challenging. Just imagine that you always knew beforehand exactly how your match was going to be played! That would eventually ruin all your pleasure and motivation.

'Friendly Eyes' and 'Good Mistakes' are the two most important pillars in training yourself to be an Action Thinker. They are the foundations of the Mindset method. Together, they create a safe basis for the remaining four pillars: curiosity, self-knowledge, self-discipline and acceptance.

PILLAR 1: FRIENDLY EYES

In our view, what stops us looking with Friendly Eyes is the dominant role of value judgments in our society. Instead of looking at yourself and the world around you judgmentally, you could try looking as an observer. Without judging immediately, you could try to observe as objectively as possible.

Looking with 'Friendly Eyes' doesn't mean glossing over your mistakes and resigning yourself to your shortcomings. It means knowing how to neutralise your emotions at the appropriate time so that they cannot disrupt your balance. This will help you to conserve energy so as to focus on the things that matter. If Zidane had reacted neutrally to Materazzi's comment in the World Cup Final, France might well have won the championship. In any case, Zidane could have bowed out of his football career with a greater sense of satisfaction. Especially when your opponent tries to provoke you or behaves obnoxiously, focusing on 'Friendly Eyes' will help you to focus on what is expected of you in the match. This will be a valuable asset.

Over the years, it has struck us that when players watch a video replay of their match they often focus only on the negative things. Reactions that we frequently hear are: 'Ugh, I look so stiff! (or awkward, slow, unathletic)' or 'Pfff, I'm playing so badly!' People just starting up as professional players do not react very differently. Their eyes ('unFriendly Eyes') can only see their shortcomings and mistakes. If they have made progress recently, they do not recognise it and it doesn't even interest them. Most players seem almost incapable of looking at themselves with 'Friendly Eyes'. For instance, pay attention to the way in which most football players criticise their own game at the end of a match (and that of teammates). They hardly pay attention to the things that went well at all.

Giving value to your efforts is an important part of Friendly Eyes. You can train yourself to have Friendly Eyes by making a habit of paying sincere compliments to yourself, your teammates, your coach, the support team and staff members.

There are so many opportunities to do so. Focussing on what went well shifts you immediately from Story Thinking to Action Thinking.

Of course, critical thinking is important, but it does not have to be linked to a negative feeling. In fact, it has been proven that neurons change in your favour when you constantly stimulate your brain in a positive way. The brain will secrete less cortisol (stress hormone) and more dopamine and serotonin (focus, happiness and calming hormones). This effects your well being and will take away some of the stress. The Friendly Eyes pillar is of great importance; it is the foundation of change.

No matter how you look at it, it is strange to call all the mistakes you make 'bad'. Can you imagine the negative impact that has on your brain's networks and how much cortisol your brain produces by doing this. Too much cortisol and adrenaline in your system will turn you into a malfunctioning machine. You can approach it differently and change which hormone your brain produces. Good Mistakes exist!

PILLAR 2: GOOD MISTAKES

The second pillar of the *Mindset* method that can help to shift you into Action Thinking and produce a balanced mindset, besides 'Friendly Eyes', is seeing your play in terms of 'Good Mistakes'. As we have already said, any change is bound to be accompanied by mistakes at first. These mistakes are actually part of the process of change. Living without making any mistakes would be about as much fun as a tea party in a graveyard. It seems clear to us that a willingness to learn from mistakes is far preferable to an attitude of leaving everything the same because it gives you a sense of security.

The concept of 'Good Mistakes' goes far beyond considering intentions more important than results. For example, your pass to a teammate or shot on goal, with the right intention, goes just wide, not exactly where you wanted it. This is a good mistake, as if you were to make the perfect pass every time, you would not be from this planet! Top athletes at the

Olympics Games indicate in interviews that they are always looking for how to learn from their mistakes. When asked what had gone wrong, their voices betrayed a striking lack of emotion. They analysed objectively what had gone 'wrong' and explained how they expected to be able to learn from this to perform better in the future. They admitted that things had not gone as they had hoped. Still, they were not angry or annoyed with themselves, since they had done what lay within their power at that time. We use this concept to bring football players into Action Thinking. For example, when you are moving up the pitch, trying to pass a player from the opposing team, you accidently kick the ball just a little too hard and lose control for a second. The player you try to pass sees that and gains control of the ball, you lose possession... that is a 'good mistake'. Why? Because this action shows a good attitude, wanting to move forward, taking risks, daring to dribble past the opponent, although the execution is not yet perfect. It is preferable to dribbling safely backwards every time and playing the ball backwards, which is often a sign of fear and insecurity.

Focusing on 'Good Mistakes' is investing in your game and good for the team in the long run. That is not to deny that a more defensive approach may sometimes be more sensible. But if you constantly adjust your game because of tension and fall back on certainties, you will never make the progress you are hoping for.

Much the same applies at a higher level. A performance level left forward, after a long sprint along the line, consistently passes her cross too short into the 16-yard area, preventing her fellow players from getting a chance for the header. She/he can choose from the three options below in this situation. Solutions 1 and 2 bring hope and therefore motivation. The player approaches herself/himself with Friendly Eyes and Good Mistakes. In solution 3, there is no hope and therefore despondency - and 'unkind eyes' - arises.

1. The left forward continues with the same tactics; she/he hopes and believes that a shift will take place, so that eventually the passes do reach the right place in the 18-yard box, right in front of the goal and her/his fellow players get a chance for the header. The left forward trusts that after several attempts, the feel for the length and height of

the pass will come. This approach to the game gives hope which keeps the motivation level high.
2. Choosing not to pass from the left to the 18-yard box, but instead dribbling inside and setting up the attack more through the middle. This change of tactics gives hope which also increases motivation.
3. Feels constant regret because the passes from the left towards the 18 yard box do not succeed. Sees no chance to escape and has no prospect of improving or changing the situation. She/he considers herself/himself a loser and this causes despondency.

'Good Mistakes' are all about effort. The point is to reward yourself for your *effort*, not for the result. Try to bear in mind that you can't do more – clearly – than 'doing your best'. The result is a separate issue. You will only make progress if you do your best. This will inevitably involve making Good Mistakes. Carol Dweck found, from conducting experiments with children and students, that they performed better when they were praised for their hard work and perseverance than when praised for their intelligence. People will nearly always achieve more when they focus on things they can control ('doing your best' and 'making the right effort') than on things over which they have no control (the result, your intelligence, and so on). This means that focusing on 'Good Mistakes' will always produce more of an improvement than focusing on the result.

You can improve the mental aspect of your game enormously if you learn to watch your own game with 'Friendly Eyes' and apply the concept of 'Good Mistakes', without constantly reproaching yourself for the mistakes you make. Often, the truth is simply that the opposing team is playing better, and instead of wallowing in self-chastisement, by retaining a spirit of curiosity, you could keep trying to find new opportunities. If you make Good Mistakes and watch yourself with 'Friendly Eyes', it will increase your self-respect. Besides enjoying yourself more in football, you will find your self-confidence growing. As a result, your relationships with your teammates and coach will improve and you will also achieve more.

Playing field or battlefield?

Emotions on the football field are frequently intense and confusing. That is partly because people are confronted with themselves and their limitations. And it is partly because when we start playing a match, we think we are doing something for fun, whereas the game frequently ends up more like a theatre of war. We hope to inspire readers to see the football field as a *playing field* rather than a *battlefield*. This will reduce tension and help you to gain more enjoyment as well as improving your game. You will be investing in yourself and your game, which will lead to progress in the long term. There is far more to be won than the match.

Winning with your team by playing in a low compact defensive organisation and hoping for a chance in the counterattack can be a very strong tactic, but it can also be very unsatisfying and feel like losing. Losing to a strong opponent while trying to apply deliberate tactics with your team, playing freely and getting the most out of yourself and the team can feel like winning.

The next table contrasts aspects of Story Thinking and Action Thinking. It is intended to provide some initial guidelines. We are talking about shifts of emphasis here, not absolute opposites.

Story Thinking	Action Thinking
past/future	now / present
judgment	observation
rationalisation	visualisation
absent	alert/focus
noise	calm
verbalisation	trigger words
technique	self-knowledge
physical	mental
holding on	letting go
consumerism	investment
tense	relaxed
control	confidence
stubbornness	flexibility
frustration	acceptance

For instance, rationalising still has a role to play in Action Thinking (though a more modest one), but visualising is the dominant mode. In Story Thinking, the emphasis is on training purely to improve technique. In Action Thinking, the emphasis shifts to developing a balanced mind by applying the pillars and concentration forms. One side-effect of this shift is that it speeds up the development of better technique.

The benefits of 'Friendly Eyes' for yourself in training or when playing a match

1. You'll feel better about your abilities and about yourself.
2. You'll feel more willing to take risks, enabling you to improve your game quicker.
3. You'll have a more objective view and therefore it will be easier to persevere.
4. Opponents will not be able to distract or affect you.

The benefits of 'Friendly Eyes' for others?

1. Your teammates, coach(es) and support staff will feel more secure in your company. This in turn will have a positive influence on their matchplay and be beneficial to your relationship with them.
2. You and your team will not feel the need to hide behind any facade, shield or armour; all subjects will be open to discussion. Even though this can be a challenge, surely openness is better than fear. Learning to trust each other matters immensely.
3. Due to this newly found openness, information will be shared quicker. In the long term this will result in even more improvement.
4. The opposing team(s) will indirectly learn that they can only win by playing better than you, due to the fact that psychological warfare does not affect you or your team.

Conclusion: putting it simply, you not only become a nicer and more satisfied person, you learn to trust others and to help each other, thus getting better results.

Can you always win?

If you really, deeply understand what is written above, you will always win the match once and sometimes twice. What we mean by this is by acting on what you have agreed to with yourself, your coach and teammates before the match and remaining respectful and committed to that plan with or without victory, you always win from yourself.

Of course, it is important to look critically, but that does not have to be linked to a negative feeling. It's a peculiar way of thinking to call all the mistakes you make 'bad', when this will constantly stimulate your brain in a negative fashion. Good Mistakes are as important as great shots!

Changing your mindset

Chapter 3 will be devoted entirely to the contrast between Story Thinking and Action Thinking. But first, in Chapter 2, we shall explore the link between pillars 3 and 4 of the *Mindset* method, curiosity and self-knowledge. A realistic self-image, only to be achieved by being curious about yourself, is essential to making a good start on changing your mindset. You can now practise Friendly Eyes and Good Mistakes by using the assignments on the following pages.

ASSIGNMENTS FOR FRIENDLY EYES

Pillar 1: Friendly Eyes when you are playing football

Make the effort to look at yourself and your teammates with Friendly Eyes for one specific match. Be aware that this is a huge challenge. As soon as you notice that you are starting to beat yourself up and/or are becoming irritated with the way you are playing, or the way your teammates are playing, look at your actions and the actions of your teammates with Friendly Eyes. That means realising that you (and your teammates) can't do more than your best and that every action is part of a learning process. You know that this learning process will help you and your team progress, which means that every action (successful or not) is part of your development. This realisation alone induces a better match mentality. If you do, you will also lift your team to a higher level. When you pay constant attention to this, you will make a profound change in your attitude on the football field. In the long run, your game will improve. Believe in it.

Pillar 1: Friendly Eyes in everyday life

For one week challenge yourself to use Friendly Eyes both at work and at home. If circumstances crop up that you feel prevent you from using Friendly Eyes realise that you have a choice. For example something happens that stops you from doing what you had set out to do, and it really makes you angry. The train is delayed, or the person who promised you something doesn't keep to the agreement. This would normally frustrate you and cause a huge energy leak. Now you decide not to fall into old patterns, you realise that you can do nothing about the situation. This time you make sure to get to the bottom of what happened, without being aggressive. And recognise that mostly people are doing their best, as you are.

People tend to emphasise the things that go wrong, which results in them becoming paralysed by external events. Focus instead on what is going well and this will free up so much mental energy.

Look at the following two examples; there is a big difference in attitude: 'All kinds of things popped up that prevented me from doing the things I wanted to do.' Or: 'Despite all of the issues that popped up, I did what was within my capabilities and didn't allow things to get on top of me. I feel so much better when I deal with situations like this.'

Friendly Eyes

By using Friendly Eyes for yourself and the opposing team, your concentration will improve dramatically.

Pillar 2: Good Mistakes when you are playing football

You may often find that you hold yourself back during a match, for fear of making mistakes. This creates problems as the pressure starts to rise. Decide instead to be more daring. If you make a mistake because you allowed yourself to try something new and bold, see it as a good mistake, because your intentions were good. These 'mistakes' are better than actions full of fear and the tensed up feeling of trying to keep everything under control. Keep your motivation high, even if you occasionally lose the ball, by repeating constantly that it was a good mistake and that you're making progress. Eventually you will learn how to strike the right balance between being taking risks and being timid.

Pillar 2: Good Mistakes in everyday life

Irritations may crop up at work or in your family, and you do nothing to change them; it's common enough. You just allow the situation to drag on in the hope that the problems will solve themselves. Unfortunately, they seldom do. Instead, take the initiative and try to communicate about these irritations, do this in a kind fashion, without blame in your voice, name the facts and also listen with an open mind, recognising that situations always have two sides to the story. If you notice that your efforts are not appreciated, don't see it as failing, but as a good mistake. Keep daring to make these kinds of Good Mistakes; don't give up. You tried to bring things up, with the best of intentions, and although it did not (yet) have the desired effect, you tried to change something unpleasant instead of just accepting the situation in passive resignation. In the end, your openness will bear fruit and make it easier to discuss things. In the long term, this will improve what you experienced as a difficult situation, even though it may not seem that way at first.

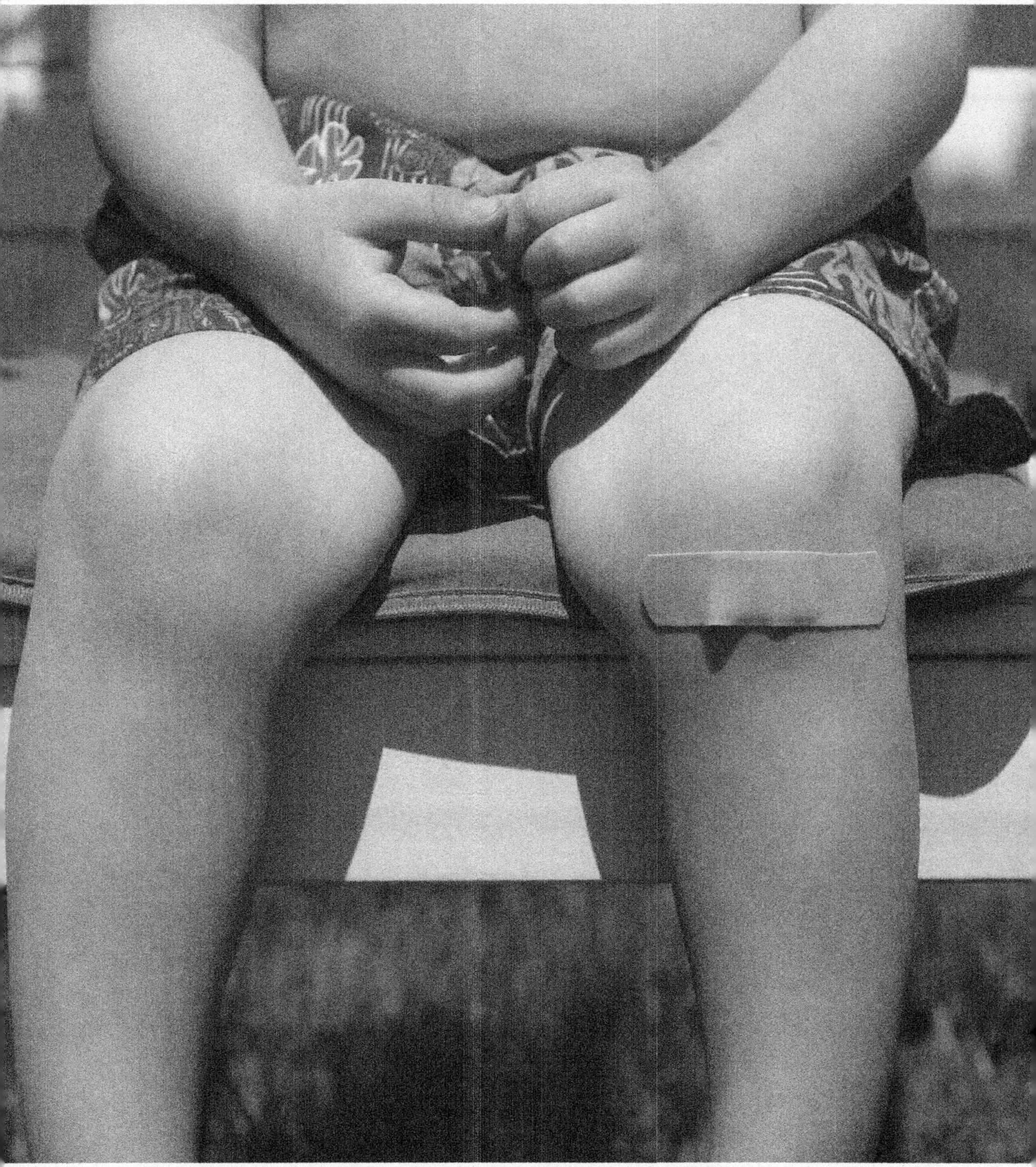

Good Mistakes

When children make mistakes, it's ok.
Treat yourself in the same fashion.

A MENTAL WARMING-UP AND COOLING DOWN

Mindset gives you and your team a practical mental structure to start and end a training session or match in Action Thinking.

MENTAL WARMING-UP

Before walking onto the pitch, mentally prepare yourself for exactly what you expect from yourself regarding your role in the team.

Do this by asking yourself the following five simple questions:
1. What do I want to achieve today? Be specific with your goals.
2. What do I want to contribute to the team? Be specific.
3. How do I want to communicate with my teammates? (Chapter 1 and the Friendly Eyes and Good Mistakes assignments can help you with this.)
4. What do I expect from my mindset/attitude?
5. What am I going to do, to remind myself to have enjoy the game?

Pay attention! If the match or training session has a *tactical* or *mental* goal, you need to decide that your full attention will be placed on that. That means that you will not be focusing on *technical* analysis of your football skills. You are investing making yourself *mentally* more resilient and gaining tactical insights.

To better understand the technical side of the mental warming-up and cooling-down we refer to Sarina Wiegman's explanation on page 10. In a *technical* training where you focus on improving your football skills, you resolve to pay attention to the specific change you want to make *technically*. If it does not yet bring the exact strategical advantage, that is understandable and important to accept. You have chosen to improve your *technique*.

In all cases, guide yourself with Friendly Eyes and Good Mistakes, and look at your teammates in the same way. Begin the training session or match with the agreements you specifically set and agreed upon for yourself and the team.

Advice:

1. If you are chatting and looking around whilst walking onto the pitch without having thought about what you expect from yourself, realise that this is a poor mental preparation.
2. If you walk onto the football pitch with an active attitude and clear goals, the training or match will start from Action Thinking.
3. Both you and your teammates take the responsibility to keep the focus on what is agreed on with each other and with the coach throughout the training/match. In this way, the coach has room to react to what exactly is occurring during the training/match, without having to worry that the players are not keeping to their own tasks and goals.
4. When you have short, clear thoughts about what you expect from yourself, you can pay much more attention to getting into the right feeling for the game and frame of mind.

MENTAL COOLING DOWN

After each match or training session ask yourself these five simple questions. Firstly, concerning yourself and then also looking at the team's all-round performance and practicing this way of cooling down together.

1. Name one specific positive point about yourself.
2. Reflect on what you have contributed to the team.
3. How was my communication with my teammates and coach?
4. Name one point that you/your teammates could improve on.
5. What gave you/your teammates enjoyment or satisfaction?

If you ask yourself and the teammates these five questions after every training session and match, you will always be able to finish on the high of Action Thinking. Be aware that it's important to remain creative when asking these questions. Crossing off the five questions after every training could become robotic. Here an example of how to change things around. When stretching at the end of the match/training you could run in pairs and ask each other the questions in this way:

1. What did you think I did well today?
2. Was there anything I did that really contributed positively to the team?
3. How did you find the way I was asking for the ball?
4. What do you think we can get better at and how?
5. Which moment in the training/match was your favourite? What was the 'ball/pass of the match?!'

When you start having conversations like this after practice sessions and matches, you will be pleasantly surprised at how insightful and pleasurable it is to communicate in this fashion. Friendly Eyes work.

The important thing is not to stop questioning. Curiosity has its own reason for existence.

ALBERT EINSTEIN

CHAPTER 2

FOOTBALL IS YOUR GAME

CURIOSITY IS A PREREQUISITE FOR SELF-KNOWLEDGE

In this Chapter you learn that you can take charge of your own progression, provided you gain insight into your real abilities.

'Only if you row to the other side of the sea will you find out who you really are', says Confucius. This is a rather tall order for most of us, but perhaps cycling to the football pitch might be enough. While you are playing a match, you will not only discover a lot about yourself, but you will also start to realise that this self-knowledge (pillar 4) is a prerequisite for improving your game. You can train as much as you like, if you don't try to acquire more self-knowledge, much of the effect will be lost. And you are the only person who can do that: *it's your game*! Perhaps we ought to turn Confucius's saying around: you can't row to the other side of the sea until you know who you really are. Because the only way to set realistic goals for yourself is to gain insight into your own abilities. Self-knowledge, attained by being curious (pillar 3), is a prerequisite for improving as a football player and it prevents you from overestimating or underestimating your own level of play. Self-knowledge is the beginning of a process in which frustration gradually gives way to acceptance and self-confidence. What will help you more than anything else to make constant progress in your game, and to enjoy doing so, is to develop a realistic self-image and to be interested in yourself. Some football players have a much too negative self-image. They feel lacking in talent and believe there is little to be done about it. Others have an unrealistic picture of themselves and imagine that they could do things that are beyond the reach of Lionel Messi. In both cases, the players leave the pitch feeling utterly demoralised.

The following sad anecdote illustrates people's tendency to leave things as they are, displaying little curiosity and shying away from change.

A woman sits at the window waiting for her husband to come home. She knows that when he returns he will be drunk and beat her. One day she sees a woman pass by who is wearing a coat that looks just like hers, and she realises with a shock that she might have been walking there herself. She goes to the hall cupboard, puts on her coat and opens the front door. When she opens the door, she recoils at all the possibilities that might present themselves in her new life. She closes the door, takes her coat off again, and takes up her old place at the window, once again waiting for her husband to come home.

Fear of the unknown or the unfamiliar can paralyse us and nip all kinds of growth in the bud. The certainty of old patterns – however destructive and frustrating they may be – seems preferable to creativity and courage and the curiosity that is needed to begin the change. How often do we see this occur in everyday life, and in sport?

In the course of her/his football career, a player constantly works on acquiring new skills. Their initial reaction is often: 'it doesn't feel right'. But what feels right and what is right may not be the same thing. The fact that something feels 'strange' does not mean that there is something wrong with it. Remember the woman in the story.

To keep making this effort, curiosity is the first and most important condition. It may be hard to imagine, but one of the things you hear most often from players of all levels after a disappointing performance is: 'I played really badly today!' Nothing else. With that attitude, you will never make any progress. Exactly what 'was bad'? Why was that? Who might help me to make some change? What does my coach think? What can I do myself to change things for the better? Only someone who displays curiosity has a real chance of improving his or her skills.

Curiosity about your own capabilities is the most important precondition for change. If you are not curious about why things keep repeating themselves, you will never be able to change them. If you think that things 'just happen to me', this arises from a lack of interest in yourself.

To consume or to invest?

What do we mean by 'consuming' and what negative effect does it have on football? Players - from beginners to professional players - often have wrong expectations of their coach and the team. They place all the responsibility on the other person, as if learning is about acquiring merchandise. Level of play cannot be bought, but your mindset can be changed, which will also improve your football. People often ask to train a lot on tactics and sometimes on technique, hoping that the football will then improve by itself.

An often-heard remark is that players can only bring about change by 'grooving their skills' during training. Many players believe that they can only make necessary changes under constant team supervision. When practising with training buddies they play without any intention. We also call this consumerism. A player who invests should constantly be busy improving themselves, also in their own off-hours, trying to make the necessary changes from *'feeling instead of thoughts'*. This will be explained later in the book.

Realise that another way of investing is also the way in which you communicate. For example when you shout 'super pass' or 'great shot' at your teammates during a match, you are raising the team to a higher level. This is establishing communication from Action Thinking. If, on the other hand, you shout 'No, not again!' or anything negative like that, you are lowering the spirit of the team and your fellow players. This is a consuming form of communication, from Story Thinking.

Another form of investing communication is daring to say what's on your mind, both to the coach and to your team. If you keep everything to yourself and only try to please everybody, this is still a form of consuming, because by not sharing your opinion you become frustrated and uncomfortable. Your coach or team will not understand what is going on inside you. In the long run this will eat away at you and your team.

Example of a club player (consumerism)

Coach: 'Kim, what do you want to work on during this 30-minute practice, in foursomes?'
(Last time Kim was feeling down after the game, so I want to give her more attention and ball contact)

Kim: 'There are some things I'm not happy about.' (I hope I will get more attention this time and really learn something.)

Coach: 'Great, give me the specifics.'

Kim: 'My direct free kick on goal from just outside the 16-metre box doesn't even go between the posts, I always shoot it two metres wide of the left post, and when I'm rushing towards the goalkeeper with the ball I just can't get past her. When I'm taking a shot I lose control of the ball, especially when someone else passes it to me with too much speed.'

Coach: 'Okay.'

Kim: 'My direct free kick is too soft by the way... It really needs to be harder. Maybe we can work on headers as well.'

Coach: 'Well we really have more than enough to work on, let's get started!'

Explanation of last remark: The coach's remark is meant sarcastically. Wanting to improve so much in one practice session is totally unrealistic. The coach chooses not to react and just wants to start the training quickly.

Example of a professional player (consumerism)

Rising star: 'Coach, thank you very much. You said that when I missed a penalty, I could rely on my skills and that I wouldn't need to think. That's the reason I missed; I should have paid attention to my technique. Your advice was completely wrong.'

Coach: 'You know that you have to invest and learn to have confidence in your skills and that it's important to pay attention to regulating your breathing. You want to develop as a player, deal with stress and join a top team, don't you?'

Rising star: 'Certainly not under your leadership, with your bad advice. I'll find another club.'

Explanation of last comment: The rising star's emotions run high after the match. Instead of realising that investing in confidence in her skills takes time, she takes no responsibility for her own fears that clearly affected her technique. She blames the coach and wants to go to another club.

The pillars: do you apply them as a consumer or as an investor?

How should the pillars be applied? Do you practise self-deception by always seeing yourself in the best possible light, or do you look honestly at how things are, instead of at how you want them to be? Experience with many *Mindset* training sessions over the years has taught us that players unconsciously put their heads in the sand when they want to change their behaviour in some fundamental way. It's important to be on your guard for this ostrich-type behaviour. Players tend to lapse into the consumer's role, and into Story Thinking when facing hard challenges about their behaviour patterns. The following paragraphs look at these two roles, consumer versus investor, and try to explain them in more detail.

People who adopt the consumer's role look for the cause of their behaviour anywhere but in themselves. While they want to change their game/behaviour, they adopt a passive attitude and expect solutions to come from outside (e.g., from the coach). Someone who adopts the role of investor, on the other hand, looks within themselves for causes ('It's your game!'). Consuming and investing are complete opposites.

Consuming / Story Thinking	Investing / Action Thinking
judgmental / hostile eyes	Friendly Eyes
unaware mistakes	Good Mistakes
indifference	curiosity
ignorance	self-knowledge
boredom	self-discipline
complacency (=passive)	acceptance (=active)

'Consumer' types, with their 'judgmental/hostile' eyes, indulge themselves and blame disappointing results on external factors (the coach, the opposing team, the umpire/referee, teammates, the wind, the pitch etc.). They are also very quick to express their opinion about everything around them; they never stop 'judging'. Investors, on the other hand, observe objectively without passing judgment. After observing they make decisions based on facts, not on emotions.

We can clearly see the difference between these two attitudes by looking at 'unaware mistakes'. Consumers tend to see all their mistakes as 'Good Mistakes' without making any mental effort to become aware and understand what they could change to improve. After all, they were simply doing their best. They don't take responsibility for their actions. Investors analyse their intentions. If the intention was good, but the way it was carried out was not perfect, it was a good mistake. But if the intention was not good (slow/timid/cowardly) the investor will look at this honestly and seek the solution within themselves, without using hostile eyes.

'Indifference' is a typical consumer-type response. It comes out in answers like 'no idea', 'I don't know' and 'yes, but'. Looking at yourself honestly and critically is alien to consumers. Displaying real curiosity by asking open questions (how does that happen, what do you think, how do you see me approaching things differently next time?) is a sign of an investor.

Consumers possess little 'self-knowledge', since they have no 'curiosity'. Consumers are therefore 'lacking awareness'.

Consumers might have 'self-discipline', but it is used to add a protective layer they need to carry on displaying consumer-type behaviour. It is the self-discipline of the man or woman who spends a fortune on diet pills without thinking of the cause of his or her excess kilos. Self-discipline where one has to take action and responsibility is considered boring or a waste of time. Taking irresponsible short-cuts is the sign of a true consumer.

A world-famous investor is the actress Julie Andrews. She says: 'Some people regard discipline as a chore. For me, it is a kind of order that sets me free to fly'.

For investors, 'acceptance' is an active step. In the case of a consumer, acceptance means complacency (passive, with little self-criticism). This entire book is about investment, and it will give many real-life examples of this mindset. The following table provides some real-life examples of consumers' behaviour.

Judgmental or hostile eyes	A player who thinks she is constantly looking at themselves with Friendly Eyes describes their match as follows: 'When I played way above my level, I realised that I would never be able to hold on to that standard for too long...'. So unconsciously this player condemns themselves to their 'normal' level. With these kind of eyes (judgmental eyes), you do not allow yourself to play very well. Another comment after the match is often: 'The other team was really annoying (unsportsmanlike, irritating, arrogant, etc.)'. If a player looks at the other team with hostile eyes, this will influence their own mindset and therefore impair their own play and concentration.
Unaware mistakes	Asked why the left midfielder dropped back deeper and deeper in the second half instead of joining in when in possession of the ball, their answer was: 'No idea, it was a difficult match for me. The ball was often passed directly to the left-winger rather than to me. You can't expect me to keep moving every time, when I only get the ball in one out of five attacks on the left.' The truth is often different: the player did not get everything out of each situation mentally and physically to always play their best.
Indifference	My fellow players pass the ball at the wrong moment to my wrong leg. This player shows no curiosity. It is important to ask the question: 'What can you do with this situation?' This involves good communication skills, so that you can make it clear how the situation can be resolved so that the ball is played onto your strong leg.

Ignorance	'I don't understand. I have done everything within my capacity to become incredibly fast, training my sprinting speed as much as possible. It is unacceptable that the other player is faster than me and can sprint pass me on their way to the goal.' There is little self-knowledge present because there is no curiosity about the deeper and mental reasons why she/he cannot solve the situation with better defensive skills or reflect on the way she/he has been practicing their sprints or any other factors that might help them to improve their speed even more.
Boredom	'We've been training four against four for weeks, it's always the same.' It is never the same, every ball is a new ball.
Complacency	During the match the player thinks: 'The ball keeps running away from me when I try to control it. I just have no feeling over the ball today. So be it, I really can't do a lot about that.' What would it be like if a heart surgeon resigned herself to 'really not caring' whilst operating? During the operation she will of course do everything to save the patient, but after the operation there is acceptance. Acceptance is something quite different than indifference.

PILLAR 4: SELF-KNOWLEDGE

The contents of your suitcase

You go to the football pitch to play a match. Compare this with going on holiday. Everything you have is in your suitcase, nothing more. If you did not have an accurate pass before leaving, you will not have it at your destination either.

We will give two examples of how a club player can deal with the contents of her 'suitcase'. Remember that football consists of four factors: **tactics, fitness, technique and mentality**.

Note: we do not claim that it is unwise to technically improve how you take a penalty (or any action); we only say that the 'consumer' often has to invest more in the mental side than she realises.

> This player is looking for a solution that is not in their suitcase
> As soon as the situation arises, the right midfielder immediately passes the high ball to the front players after taking it with the inside of their foot. Unfortunately, her/his pass is only precise about 20% of the time. The right midfielder decides to do something that is not in her/his suitcase, she/he takes the ball with the outside of her/his foot and passes it as quickly as possible. This results in less control over the ball and even more ball loss, because this skill is not in her/his suitcase.
> After the match, the right midfielder decides to train for a week on taking high balls with the outside of their foot, but in the next match this skill is still not in their suit- case and a lot of ball loss happens yet again.
>
> What does this player do when they realise that their suitcase has less content than they think?
> After the second match, the player decides to talk to the coach who also understands the mental side of football.
> The coach suggests that the player be more realistic with what they already have in their suitcase. First work on improving her passes with the inside of the foot. Then pay attention to ball control and taking a little bit more time to get the ball ready before it is played. Even if it takes a little longer for the ball to be passed, there is more ball control and more balls will arrive precisely at her teammates feet, which will also give the player more self-confidence.
>
> Insight
> Naturally, the player would also like to take the high ball with the outside of her/his foot, make it ready for play and pass it on quickly. However, it takes time to get this skill into your suitcase and rushing things will cause loss of confidence and that in turn often brings frustration and anger and thus even more loss of the ball.

In the long term it will pay dividends to change your technique and use the new skills in matches, but this is a long process that requires patience and perseverance. The point we are making here is simply that what feels right and what is right are two different things at that moment in time. During matches you need to have an acceptance of your actual capabilities. A long period of investment after the match will be needed to boost development further, not just a couple of weeks.

Showing respect for your opponent and acquiring self-knowledge

The determination to win a match at any price may blind you and distort your assessment of your own strength, that of your teammates and that of the opposing team. Understanding yourself in every aspect of your game also means being able to assess your own strength in relation to that of your teammates and your opponents. If you lose a match, your opponents were the better team at that point, that is all there is to it. Often players who have lost a match frequently show too little respect for the other team. By constantly making excuses or belittling your opponents you will ultimately undermine your self-respect.

> Example of a club player (someone who lacks a realistic image of her own strength and has no respect for the other team):
> 'Pfff. As a striker I hardly got the ball in this match. The other team plays with so many players behind the ball, we couldn't get through. That's no way to play football, I get an occasional high ball in front of the goal but I can't do anything with it. I don't mind losing to a better team, but losing to a team that only defends is really frustrating.'
>
> Example of a competitive or professional player (someone who lacks a realistic image of her own strength and has no respect for the other team):
> 'It's always the same against that team. I have to face the same fast right-winger who I just can't keep up with. But you know what, I never want to be a player who only relies on speed, when so many other skills are just as important.'

Stages of learning

Let's look at the process of gaining more insight into your own capabilities. The following table is often used for the different phases of learning.

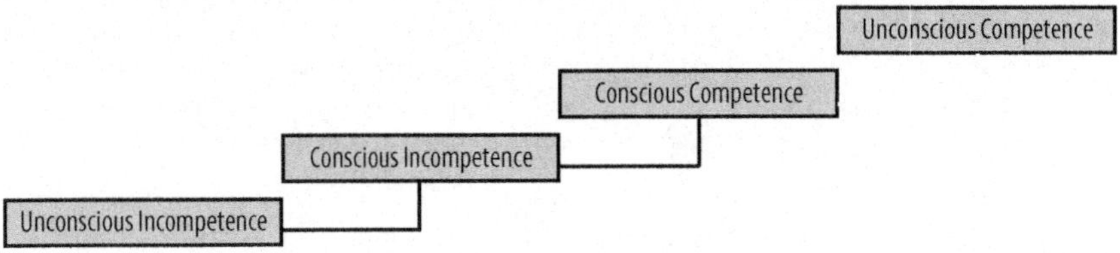

A player who has a good grasp of this process will approach her development in a far more conscious way. She will constantly have to go back to the table and keep applying it to each part of her game to reach a higher level.

In general, this is the meaning of the different stages:

Unconscious Incompetence (UI): you don't know you can't do something. You are unaware of not having the skill.

Conscious Incompetence (CI): you know you can't do something. You are aware that you do not possess the skill yet.

Conscious Competence (CC): you can do something if you really concentrate. If you are consciously aware you are mostly capable of mastering the skill.

Unconscious Competence (UC): you can do something well without having to think about it (reflex). You are instinctively master of the skill.

The following examples are based on a match situation. We could easily come up with dozens of other examples, at any level of play, but this example will quickly clarify what the terms in the table mean in a practical situation.

	Unconscious Incompetence	Conscious Incompetence	Conscious Competence	Unconscious Competence
Mentality	Mentality, what's that got to do with football?	I always seem to have a negative attitude on the pitch.	If I find myself getting negative, I can usually catch myself in time and turn it around into a positive attitude.	People say that I always seem positive and dynamic on the pitch.
Tactics	It's great keeping the ball in my possession as long as possible, it's a pity that I usually lose the tackle at some point.	When I pass the first player, I totally lose sight of where my teammates are.	If I concentrate well, I manage to look around me after a pass and regularly play the ball accurately forward.	After passing the player covering me, I feel when the moment's right to pass to a teammate or to continue driving forward.
Fitness	Football really isn't a strenuous sport. I never get tired on the pitch.	Football is so strenuous; I'm always exhausted in the second half.	If I go running once a week and do my interval training, I still feel fit in the second half.	My teammates tell me that they love that I'm still so fit at the end of the second half.
Technique	I don't understand why my technique doesn't hold up when I shoot on goal. I train this shot so often.	Due to the fact that I often pull my upper body backwards too quickly, I sometimes shoot too high.	When I become aware of the position of my upper body, I can usually adjust the height of my shot.	I can take a pretty accurate shot on goal whenever I want.

The examples illustrate mentality, tactics, fitness, and technique, in that order. 'Unconscious incompetence' can be quite funny!
Here is an anecdote that everyone will recognise. Try to decide which of the above boxes it belongs in. Is the player at the stage of conscious competence, conscious incompetence or unconscious incompetence, and in which elements of the game (mentality, tactics, fitness, technique)?

Club player

'Julian's game is weak; he thinks he can get past me all the time. I will show him what real defending in football is. If he tries to pass me one more time I will take the ball right off him. I'll give it all I've got! That eternal pinging of his! Right, I'm going to go in like a bull and stick my right leg out to get that ball! Oops.... The ball goes past me. Never mind, to make up for it I'll try a sliding... pity too late. A bit too enthusiastic.'

The answer is that this player is at the stage of unconscious incompetence in all areas: mentality, tactics, fitness and technique.

What are the causes underlying this player's unconscious incompetence? Let's look at each area in turn. UI=Unconscious Incompetence.

UI mentality: overestimates his own abilities; is busy judging his opponent instead of concentrating on the ball. (Julian's game is weak)

UI tactics: impatient, the choice was to try to take the ball away immediately rather than wait for the attacker to let the ball get further away from his feet or wait until you yourself were covered in the back by another defender.

UI fitness: physically insufficiently wide, low and on the front of his feet (read: insufficiently trained to be capable to move at the necessary speed.)

UI technique: lacks the movement skills to move with the attacker in all directions and make impact at the right time. The body is too high and the weight is not on his front feet.

If you recognise problems in your game, in any area, you have already taken the first, important step in the right direction, since you have gone from unconscious incompetence to conscious incompetence. Sometimes this does not feel particularly good at the time, but that will change, you are opening doors to improvement.

Our method aims at consciousness-raising, with the ultimate aim of playing unconsciously. 'Unconscious competence' in football means playing instinctively.

To actually set change in motion and to accomplish it calls for creativity and courage. For the time being, it is sufficient to know that it means breaking with old habits. For example, players say: 'Everyone knows that I am a fierce defender.' However, sometimes in a one-on-one situation, a lot of patience is required before stepping in to take the ball away. Being patient does not mean that you are not a fierce defender, but that you have a deeper understanding of the game. A player who lacks this flexibility will find it hard to make the transition from being consciously incompetent to consciously competent and ultimately unconsciously competent.

Pillar 3: Curiosity during football related to myself
When you're talking to your coach or teammates, do you sometimes find yourself answering with 'yes, but'? 'Yes, but' is the opposite of curiosity. If you notice yourself doing this, try saying instead: 'Yes, and how do you think things might be different?' The same applies to responses like 'I don't know.' This answer doesn't show much curiosity or encourage conversation. Form your own opinion or if you really don't know how to answer, say 'Can you help me understand?'

Pillar 3: Curiosity during football related to the opposing team
During a match we are often riddled with judgmental thoughts about the other team. Their tactics are annoying you. You could change your approach to these judgments by becoming curious about your reaction to your opponents game, by asking yourself: what is so challenging about this type of tactics and what can I do?

Pillar 3: Curiosity in everyday life
Really listen to the person you're talking to. This may sound obvious, but if you pay attention, you'll notice that you might spend more time interpreting than actually listening. You might fill everything in, because you already have a picture of the person. Make a determined decision to actively listen, not to interrupt or fill in the gaps. What is the person actually saying? Ask more questions or just be silent, if something is not entirely clear. You can ask open questions like: 'What do you mean?' or: 'What would you do if...?' You'll notice that you are rewarded with other people's surprising and original ideas, which you would otherwise have missed.

Use these words to begin an open question:
How? (asking about a way of doing things, or a method);
What? (asking about the meaning and content);
When, how long, how often? (asking about time);
Where, where to? (asking about a place);
Why, because of what, in what respect? (asking about cause).
Who, which? (asking about the subject).

Curiosity

It might be a little bit scary to take a closer look, but it's also exhilarating!

Pillar 4: Self-knowledge

We all go through 'moods' of Action Thinking and Story Thinking. If you're in a mood like this, how would you score in the various different components? Grade yourself from 1 to 5 (1 = never, 5 = always). It is possible to have high (or low) scores in two opposing categories. For instance, if you score low in Story Thinking and high in Action Thinking for a specific component, this is generally a strength. If the score is the other way round, in other words high in Story Thinking and low in Action Thinking, this may be an area that needs improvement.

The point of this assignment is to improve your self-knowledge. Ask your coach, teammate or colleague to fill in the table for you as well, that feedback will help you form a realistic picture of yourself.

Story Thinking	1	2	3	4	5	Action Thinking	1	2	3	4	5
judgmental eyes						*Friendly Eyes*					
unaware mistakes						*Good Mistakes*					
indifference						*curiosity*					
ignorance						*self-knowledge*					
boredom						*self-discipline*					
complacency						*acceptance*					
negative						positive					
insecure						self-confident					
giving up						persevering					
impatient						patient					
full of doubt with						conviction					
apathetic						motivated					
stubborn						flexible					
fearful						courageous					
predictable						creative					
dependent						autonomous					
easily distracted						focused					

6 Pillars

Self-knowledge

Is the truth always what you see in the mirror? To find out: ask your coach, teammates, family or friends.

WHAT ARE THE RIGHT INGREDIENTS TO MAKE A COMPLETE TEAM?

The start of a 'complete team' is finding motivated and disciplined players and a coach with vision and compassion. The next step is to make clear agreements with all involved; the coach, players and support team, on certain basic principles that we would like to invite you to consider in this Intermezzo.

At the highest level of the game, it is necessary to be surrounded by an array of experts. Such as a video analyst, a physical trainer, a physiotherapist, a dietician, a goalkeeping coach, a sports psychologist, organisational staff, and to have the practical and financial resources to make a professional complete team possible. Fortunately, by keeping to a few clear guidelines, all teams can create a professional atmosphere with a brilliant mindset. We often think that money will make the difference but this is not necessarily true.

The ingredients for a complete team

1. Everyone is motivated and enthusiastic—the coach, your teammates, the physical trainer and all of the support team. Friendly Eyes and Good Mistakes are applied. A great coach together with the staff and the team, give four times more positive feedback than critical feedback. Things that need to be improved on are addressed from 'encouragement to grow' and 'curiosity', not from 'you need to do that better'. As soon as you notice that the coach or fellow players approach things more often than not in a negative way, or put huge pressure on each other in a pressing fashion, than have the courage to discuss this.
2. Discussion is allowed and no one is scared of criticism. Both staff and players dare to speak out, give their views and also dare to share vulnerabilities.
3. Listening is active and open questions are asked. Players are encouraged to come up with their own solutions.

4. When complex decisions have to be made, the coach takes full responsibility, confronts others when necessary, makes the decisions and communicates what and why has been decided to all and acts appropriately.
5. The coach regularly asks the team for feedback on her/his advice.
6. Everyone is involved in each other's play and progress in all areas; players are not put on a pedestal.
7. Everyone is always on time for appointments and training sessions are never cancelled without a clear reason.
8. When target-oriented and specific practice exercises and assignments are given for independent training, the players take responsibility to execute them with great attention and without guidance.
9. During training sessions and matches both the coach, support staff and players keep talking to the minimum, meaning that no long stories or explanations are needed on the pitch. They focus on choosing words that are to the point and matter for the progress of the team. They know how important concentration is and realise that their stories can wait until a more appropriate moment.
10. There needs to be a common vision of what the team is working towards. A clear course is set for the short and long term, which is not only result oriented but above all task oriented.
11. A player who intends to change teams or to quit, first announces this to the coach, gives the reasons for their decision and thanks the coach for their effort. Only then does she inform the other players.
12. A coach who decides to suspend a player shall first inform the individual player of their decision and the reasons. Only after this has been done, are the other players informed.
13. Everyone involved is constantly working on team development. The coach, players and support staff are willing to seek and hire external help when they feel they are not making the progress they are striving for. If there is a lack of funds, then sponsored walks or runs could create possibilities.

It might sometimes feel overwhelming to create a complete team, but it is imperative to think about what such a team could look like and to realise that your behaviour is always a building block in its formation. Your mental preparation and commitment is solely dependent on yourself.

ASSIGNMENTS FOR ALL TO BECOME PART OF A COMPLETE TEAM

What role can you play?

Read the seven statements below and give yourself points from 1 to 10. 1 is the lowest and 10 is the highest. By doing this, you will gain self-knowledge and you can discuss the points with your coach and teammates. In this way, you can all set goals to make progress and make the team more complete.

1. I keep to my appointments both on and off the field.
2. I am always on time for training. This means that all of my equipment is ready before I go to the training/match and that my mindset is focused on what I expect of myself and what is expected of me.
3. I give positive feedback to both my coach and teammates when something works.
4. I'm clear when something doesn't work and I come up with concrete examples based on facts, not on emotions, to clarify what's not going well and try to formulate how the situation could improve.
5. I show one hundred per cent physical and mental commitment during training and matches.
6. I do the mental warming up and cooling down as described in 'Intermezzo 1'.
7. I arrange all business matters correctly and clearly. I think about what terms have been agreed upon. What is in my contract with the English football association and/or my club? What has been agreed upon regarding social media? I stick to my agreements and treat everyone with respect.

It takes time and energy to forge the team into a whole, where everyone knows and grows into their role. According to Sarina Wiegman; 'You don't win a tournament with eleven players. You need the whole team and everyone knew what was expected from her when we (the technical staff) had to make a change, and everyone had trust that this would make a difference. Every single player accepted her role.'

When a man is sufficiently motivated, discipline will take care of itself.

ALBERT EINSTEIN

CHAPTER 3

PLAYING FOOTBALL WITH A BEARD

THE BALLAST OF THINKING TOO MUCH

This Chapter provides insight into the origins of your fear and insecurities and teaches how you can start to overcome them.

Many people start it as soon as they wake up and are still going strong when they lie down to go to sleep: they are editing a film in their heads. The film is made up of thoughts and emotions related to their past and future. It is rattling on incessantly, even on the football field. That is what we call Story Thinking, and the metaphor we use for it is the *malfunctioning machine*. Once we have achieved *presence of mind*, this mode of thought no longer applies; its place has been taken by Action Thinking. Action Thinking focuses on the 'now'. The player has managed to banish all distracting thoughts and is fully immersed in the moment. This is not something that can be done at the drop of a hat. It requires years of concentrated effort, a process of trial and plenty of mistakes. This book essentially provides a mental plan, a series of stages towards attaining the 'now'. The result is what happens to a football player in top form giving a perfect assist – exactly as they had seen it in their mind before they actually executed it. This is called visualisation. The point is that you feel and see instinctively beforehand what is going to happen, and it does.

Many readers will remember the legendary goal that Marco van Basten scored against the Soviet Union in the final of the 1988 European Football Championship. It was one of the finest goals of all time. In a TV documentary, Van Basten explains that his strike was no coincidence. His shot at goal was carefully 'aimed and timed'. Closer analysis reveals that the ball soared about ten centimetres above the hands of Dasayev, the best keeper in the tournament, and dipped five centimetres below the crossbar. An almost impossible achievement. Van Basten explained that when Mühren passed the ball to him, the insight came to him (in… sight = visualisation) that it was possible.

Comparable to Van Basten's performance was the magnificent goal scored by Alessia Russo for England, in the win over Sweden in the semi-final of the 2022 Women's European Championships. From an awkward position in the penalty area, surrounded by other players, and with her back to the goal, she scored backwards with her heel, right into the little space that was there.

Russo: 'It was very instinctive. I didn't have time to think much about it. I just knew that I wanted to get another shot off while the ball was still so close to the goal. I think there was a player in front of me, so I couldn't have turned because I would have got myself into trouble there. So yeah, I had to decide how I could get the ball in the net as quick as possible and the back of my heel was just the quickest route to go.' As in the case of Van Basten, there was no 'rational' decision, but Russo instinctively felt what she had to do.

PLAYING FOOTBALL WITH A BEARD

In his essay collection *Het sadistische universum* ('The sadistic universe', 1964), the Dutch novelist W.F. Hermans recalls an anecdote about a man with a remarkably fine beard from Alphonse Allais's story 'La barbe'. One day, a girl asks this proud owner of one of the most magnificent beards in Paris whether he sleeps with his beard inside his blanket or on top of it. The poor man has never given the matter a moment's thought. That night, when he goes to bed, he can't sleep. He lays his beard on top of the blanket, then puts it underneath, but he just can't fall asleep. He parts his beard in two, placing some above and some below the blankets, but in vain. However much he manoeuvres his beard, his confusion and compulsive thoughts keep getting worse and worse, and he is totally incapable of sleep.

Hermans goes on to comment that one can easily guess how the man finally ends his torment, after a long series of sleepless nights. The only solution remaining to him is a visit to the barber. The radical removal of his beard will finally solve his insomnia.

The radical removal of Story Thinking is the only way in which we can solve our problem of tensing up, 'choking' and over-consciousness. Unfortunately, most active participants in sport, at all levels, think too much. This is a form of ballast which undermines our enjoyment and our performance.

To let this really sink in, let's take another look at the table printed in Chapter 1. Many of the contrasts will now have become far clearer.

Story Thinking	Action Thinking
past / future	now / present
judgment	observation
rationalisation	visualisation
absent	alert/focus
noise	calm
verbalisation	trigger words
technique	self-knowledge
physical	mental
holding on	letting go
consumerism	investment
tense	relaxed
control	confidence
stubbornness	flexibility
complacency	acceptance
ego	being

The last contrast on the list needs a little explanation. The ego is a breeding ground for stories, and the ego lives on stories. It constantly feeds and defines itself by Story Thinking. Without this thinking it would evaporate, and the ego is so constructed that it will do anything to avoid this fate. That is why it is so hard to reach the storyless 'now' – to achieve 'just being', as Buddhists say. Everyone knows the phenomenon of 'grumbling at yourself': this is the ego blatantly at work. Ego and Story Thinking are the two sides of one medal. But not of the medal you can win in a tournament, since they lead only to frustration, loss of concentration, and as a result to poorer play. The ego verbalises, rationalises and judges. It is fondest of mechanisms that strengthen it, like commenting, criticising and complaining. These magnify the ego, but they also magnify your sense of frustration. The ego benefits from frustration and anger. There are tried and tested ways of silencing the ego and the buzzing mosquitoes of Story Thinking whilst playing football: concentrate on your breathing, visualisation, positive reinforcement ('trigger words'), awareness of where your eyes are (eye control) and developing rituals. These techniques and more will be explained in detail in Chapters 5 and 6.

Thinking with your body

Let's go back to the player who plays a perfect assist. They have seen precisely beforehand (visualisation) where they want to play the ball. It just happens. This is sometimes called 'flow': it happens when the mind is free of thought and has changed into pure, non-judgmental observation. Inner noise has been replaced by a sense of calm. Mind (thought) and body (action) come together. The state of flow is that of continuous direct observation, without judgment or bias. You could also call it 'total presence' or 'total alertness'. It expresses itself in a perfect sense of ease on the football pitch. Players often experience flow during training sessions. That is because there is no emotional attachment to the score, as there is in a match. It is a *playing-field* situation, not a *battlefield*. You might say that in this state, football is a dynamic form of meditation: it is played in the 'now' without judgments or fears intervening to muddy the experience.

Why do players often enjoy training sessions more than matches?

Perhaps it has now become clear why training is often so much more fun than playing matches, and why you often play so much better in them. In matches, past and future may play a prominent role (Story Thinking). Training sessions generally take place in the now (Action Thinking). Action Thinking is thinking with your body; the aim is to deactivate the process of rational thinking, leaving the action to the body, the subconscious. This means, for instance, deploying technique *unconsciously* rather than *consciously*. We need to develop a child's relationship to our body, learning playfully and applying what we have learned.

Of course, this only applies when you are, for example, 'sharpening' your skills, not when you are changing your technique. If you are working on controlling with the inside foot of both legs over a short distance, to gain more ball control, then you can let your body completely 'unconsciously' do its job.

On the other hand, if you want to improve your skills with your instep over longer distances, you will first have to be aware of placing your standing leg and/or where exactly you hit the ball on the foot.

The aim should be to make the switch from conscious to unconscious as fast as possible. Once you are working in Action Thinking, your body has an opportunity to perform its movements in a smooth and relaxed way. If you are 'over-conscious' of the position of your foot, you are in Story Thinking, and the movement will feel uncomfortable and wooden.

Making the mental switch from Story to Action Thinking will fundamentally transform your experience and your level of play during a match. It will also affect your progress in training sessions.

What are the specific consequences of this change of mindset on the football pitch?

What many players do not realise is that performing is linked to an extremely complex mental state. People will often say; 'Oh really, that's just a question of improving your technique!' 'Surely an inaccurate long pass just means you need to practise more to improve your technique?' *No, the technical execution of a long pass is influenced by the player's mental state.* What can happen, for example, in the mind of a player who gives a long ball? She thinks about position and technical aspects such as: do I have enough space to pass, do I take it with the inside of the foot or instep, where do I put my standing leg, how should my upper body position be, how far do I swing my leg through, and so on.

This is a useful approach when training elements of technique, but in a match it may easily ruin your accuracy. There is a considerable risk that this 'over-consciousness thinking' may adversely affect the long ball during a match. This is Story Thinking. The player can prevent it by visualising the path the ball will follow and the exact spot where it will hit the ground. Depending on their level, the player visualises the pass and banishes all aspects of technique (which training sessions have put 'in their system' – the 'suitcase' in Chapter 2) from their mental preparation for the pass. This will greatly increase the likelihood of them producing a successful pass. This is Action Thinking. And if the player misses after all, they find it far easier to accept, which means they have a much better chance of succeeding the next time they encounter exactly the same situation. In this case, the player will experience it as a 'good mistake'.

PILLAR 5: SELF-DISCIPLINE

To change your mindset, you need both self-discipline and courage. Everyone who reads the following paragraphs will see that the arguments they contain are plain common sense. The only way of making a concrete change to your mindset is with a healthy dose of self-discipline and working with a clear mental goal (see Chapter 9).

'I don't dare' – what does that mean?

Players often say that having had a particular pass or action in mind, they found that they 'didn't dare' to actually execute it. However, convinced they may have been that this particular pass or action was the right one, they lacked the courage to follow through. That is because they were already preparing a negative outcome in their minds – 'suppose I lose the ball'. Since they are not in the here and now of Action Thinking, but in the future of Story Thinking: because they are not visualising but rationalising, they tense up and are no longer capable of completing the action that was intended. The malfunctioning machine takes over from the *presence of mind*. With heightened self-discipline the player can conjure up the right choice at the right moment. You can decide to be daring. Also, if the player is prepared to release attachment to the score it will help her achieve her best standard at every given moment.

Attachment to the score

We were 1-0 down. As a central defender, I regularly got a lot of space in front of me but I kept playing the ball square. I couldn't believe it, I kept doing it, I tensed up completely and didn't dare to dribble in and build up, which would have created more chances and we then we might have won.

How often do you hear stories like that? Many teams have lost matches by tensing up as a result of being fixated on the score. It is good to remember that you should always be playing for the next forward action, passing action, defensive action, safe action etc. and never for the half-time or final score. Bear in mind that the score can indeed influence tactics. For example, when you have a big lead, you can take more risks.

But this is quite separate from becoming fixated on the score. That is what we mean here by 'attachment': the score becomes a 'story' that dominates the game.

Forget the score and concentrate on the only action that matters: the one you're executing now. Whenever you find yourself thinking of the score during the match, try to put those thoughts aside. The Instruments described in Chapter 6 will help you make this step. As soon as you start focusing on the score, you lapse into Story Thinking, which will undermine your concentration.

What often happens if you have a strong attachment to someone? You start worrying that something may happen to him or her. All sorts of horror scenarios loom up if the person does not turn up on time. This is Story Thinking in its full-blown form. Everyone knows the negative influence of these pointless thoughts. Although it may seem far-fetched to compare this to an attachment to the score in a match, in fact exactly the same mechanism is at work here. This attachment gives rise to stories that undermine your concentration and mental balance. 'If only I hadn't…', 'Now I must really take care not to…', 'I wish I had never…'; everyone has had thoughts like this during a match. They cause you to tense up. You want to intercept a ball but you feel glued to the spot, you want to shoot a powerful free kick but your striking leg feels heavy and doesn't seem to be able to swing through the ball, you stumble over the ball whilst attempting to go past the opponent. Being attached to the score can paralyse you, and can cause you to 'choke'. You must learn to let go.

Letting go

'Letting go' is not denial but acceptance. You should not invest mental energy in things that you cannot influence. Don't become irritated about things that are unavoidable but accept them. The first step is to become conscious of the irritation. Try to see that irritation as a feeling that crops up, but don't identify with it. In other words, it is not part of your personality, your ego. It is simply something that comes your way, so that you can decide what to do with it. You are not identified with the irritation and so you can look at it from a distance. It is pointless to worry about what others think of you, about whether you are coming up to your own expectations, or about things that you have no power to change.

If you can't influence something, you need to learn to let it go. Don't blame things you can't influence, or which are just as annoying for your opponent as for yourself. If you do, you will only disrupt your balance and generate 'noise' in your head – Story Thinking – and your performance will suffer as a result.

What others say

During tournaments, it is essential that you largely shut yourself off from the outside world. Leah Williamson says about this that during the European Championships: 'We never paid attention to what people were saying or what was going on outside. We kept it out first so we never heard most of it but if anything crept in, we really weren't focused on it.'

Part of Story Thinking is when you let what is written on social media, in the press or said on TV about you, your coach or your team influence you. Many great performers switch off all social media channels and do not watch or listen to the news whilst in 'performance mode'. That way there is no chance of them being distracted or influenced in a way that might affect their game. Self-discipline in these matters can make a day and night difference in the way you feel.

Things that you can't influence – and which might distract you into Story Thinking:

- the role of the media and social media;
- the weather;

- the football pitch; the surface, the lines, the space, the surroundings, the lights;
- the stands;
- the changing rooms;
- the dug-outs;
- noises and other distractions outside the field;
- your opponent's behaviour: how they push against you, how they execute a tackle, how they shout (or don't shout), where they stand, how they look, what they say, what clothes they are wearing;
- your opponent; the type of passes she/he gives, how she/he receives the ball (you sometimes have an influence on this);
- the behaviour of the spectators; who they are, whether they are partisan, the language they use, how loud they talk, how much they move, how they clap and cheer only for your team or the other team;
- the referee's decisions;
- the decisions of the coach;
- the quality of the ball (in a competition or tournament situation)

Things that you can influence
– and that promote Action Thinking:

- your own material - ensuring it is well prepared beforehand: your shoes, socks, shin pads, your haircut, your bag, spare laces, trigger words at hand;
- ensuring that you have something to eat and drink with you;
- your personal task and pre-made goals aligned with the game plan of the team;
- your recovery time on the pitch is influenceable - (see Chapter 7: Tactics are based on feeling);
- your breathing/heart rate in different situations - (see Chapter 7: Tactics are based on feeling);
- your preparation for the match: training, bedtime, diet, visualisation;
- your commitment;
- motivating your fellow players according to Friendly Eyes and Good Mistakes.

Once it becomes clear in your mind what you can let go of, everything becomes rather easier to handle. It is quite incredible how many things people can get wound up about. If you dare to let things go, you will be able to get the best out of yourself, and influence your team in a positive way.

To learn more about this and to practise this, go to Intermezzo 3.

A question that is often asked:
'Why am I simply incapable, again and again, of mustering the necessary discipline? I always seem to revert to the same old patterns as before.'

The answer to this question is:
Most people want a quick fix and become disheartened when they cannot sustain their progress and don't immediately get the great results they want. They become impatient, judgmental and fall back into old patterns.

This attitude is devastating, as you do not give yourself the credits for the effort and improvement you are making. By becoming conscious of the journey you are on and the benefits you will gain in the long run, you become a much more balanced athlete and person. This will give you the energy needed to carry on. Your consistency, patience and investment will produce a concrete shift from story thinking to action thinking. Learn to enjoy the process of change, instead of only longing for 'the results'.

Pillar 5: Self-discipline during football

Over the next two weeks, maintain a constant awareness of your breathing during training sessions and matches; pay attention to how it changes when you're under pressure, and after a particular action. Of course, your physical effort has a great impact, but what we are guiding you to do is to become more aware of the psychological aspect of your breath. For instance: after a really tough action, take the time to slow your breathing down before starting a new action. For clear instructions on this subject, see the section on 'breathing' in Chapter 6, where we discuss exactly how best to deal with your breathing. If you can muster the discipline to raise your awareness of your breathing for two weeks, we can guarantee that you will recover from each action more rapidly and be ready to start the next one from a more present state of mind.

Pillar 5: Self-discipline in everyday life

Make sure that all the right conditions are in place before starting a performance moment. That may sound easy and obvious, but our experience with professionals as well as athletes, often shows the opposite.

We suggest that you stick to the following plan. Make sure that all your preparations have been taken care of in advance of your performance. In general, people know perfectly well what these essential preparations are, but all too often they leave things to the last minute. This causes a sense of agitation at the beginning, for instance at an interview, important meeting, an exam or a match. If you improve your discipline in this area, it will help you to achieve a greater sense of inner calm. This assignment may sound rather simple, but we know from experience that it is often underestimated and it is necessary to help to get you off to your best performances.

Self-discipline

'Some people regard discipline as a chore. For me, it is a kind of order that sets me free to fly.'

JULIE ANDREWS

I speak to everyone in the same way, whether he is the garbage man or the president of the university.

ALBERT EINSTEIN

CHAPTER 4

LIFE VERSUS FOOTBALL

WHAT YOU CAN'T HIDE WHEN PLAYING FOOTBALL

This Chapter makes it clear why football has such a strong psychological component, involving a head-on confrontation with yourself

Coach José Mourinho speaks in an interview about one of his former players at Inter Milan, the renowned enfant terrible Mario Balotelli. The story is about a match they played in the Champions League against Rubin Kazan. All of Inter Milan's strikers were injured, the only striker Mourinho had left was Balotelli. In the 43rd minute, he receives a yellow card. Mourinho takes him aside at half-time. He keeps talking to him for 14 of the 15 minutes and urges him not to touch anyone in the second half, only the ball. 'If you lose the ball, no reaction. When someone provokes you, no reaction. If the referee make a mistake, no reaction. Please Mario...' In the 46th minute, Balotelli gets a red card. Mourinho says he sees this and many other incidents mainly as comical. Both off the football pitch and during matches, the striker was an unfocused bomb about to explode, who cared little for advice from others and took no responsibility. That, in retrospect, Mourinho saw this behaviour as comical is quite generous and at the same time, what becomes clear is that it is extremely difficult to manage a player with such a character. Ultimately, the right concentration and attitude has to come from the player himself. He has to take responsibility and deal with the traits he also has in everyday life. These qualities are often magnified on the football pitch, because they cannot be disguised there.

Another important part of this anecdote that needs to be mentioned concerns the 14-minute conversation at half time with only one player! This we believe is out of all proportion. For the rest of the team, only one minute remained for the coach to discuss strategy with them or to give them mental support and guidance. One person caused the coach to neglect the entire team.

It is often the case that players whose attitude and/or play is substandard move the responsibility towards everything other than themselves. Why is that? That has everything to do with the confusion of 'performance' and 'reality'. If a performer has a certain idea of their own ability that is not based on reality, they will not be able to believe that their underperformance is due to their own doing. The player will automatically start looking for all kinds of external reasons and excuses, rather than looking honestly into the mirror. In the examples below, Lucy always puts her own story above what is actually going on. She does not want to accept reality; this leads to excuses, blame, frustration and even worse play. Always keep the following in mind, which is also one of the punch lines of this book: Football is your game! You are responsible and in control!

What and who does Lucy blame?

Blame: No support from teammates

The striker Lucy plays in a team with a really fast right winger with an accurate pass. Lucy is strong and confident in ball possession with close control in the square meter and usually positions herself well in the 18-yard box. She doesn't have a strong header.

The right winger has been given the task of running from the far sideline to the touch-line and getting close to the 18-yard box before giving a low cross for goal.

The right winger passes her defender and dribbles the ball towards the touch-line. From just outside the 18-yard box, she delivers a low cross in

front of goal. Lucy, the striker, cannot control the ball and the opponent's defence manages to gain possession and clear the ball. Lucy starts to shout at the right winger 'give a better cross next time, you messed up again!' Lucy points to her forehead and shakes her head at the right winger.
The blame certainly does not lie with Lucy, but of course with the right winger.

Blame: Again no support from teammates

On the counter attack, Lucy has possession of the ball and dribbles towards the 18-yard box, the rest of the team advances with her. Everyone does their utmost to position well in front of the goal. Lucy tries to pass the central defender and loses the ball. Lucy shouts to her teammates, with great annoyance in her voice: 'And what kept you guys?'
The blame now lies with the whole team, certainly not with Lucy!

Own fault, but self-hatred

Lucy comes off the pitch defeated. She was substituted in the middle of the second half because she could no longer get past her defender and was regularly losing the ball. 'I was out there playing against myself. After my actions in front of the goal in the first half didn't result in a goal, I started cramping up. Didn't even get a shot on goal. I'm really in need of therapy. How is it possible? Passing a defender is normally my strength. If I can't do that anymore, I better stop. I hate myself and I hate playing matches and I hate football!'
No one, including Lucy, needs to take the blame in this way. Today it apparently didn't go that well, apply Friendly Eyes and Good Mistakes, they will help you to keep going. It's all part of the game, be kind to yourself.

These are examples of a club player. But players of all standards will be able to identify with some of these points in their own struggle.
In fact, problems are even more likely to become more obvious when competing in football than in everyday life, where it is usually possible to hide your weak points temporarily. Out on the field, you'll be found out straight away. Players who are capable of developing rapid insight into their reactions, and can manage to break away from negative patterns of behaviour, will generally be able to apply the same abilities off

the football pitch too. In other words, changing the way you compete can actually improve your life in other ways. During a match, problems that exist in your everyday life are often revealed in a concentrated form, unconcealed and blatantly obvious. Players frequently lose their self-respect while playing a match (lose their courage or nerve). Research has shown that self-respect primarily comes down to one thing. What do you do if you are faced with a difficult situation? Face it, tackle it and take action, or turn away, avoid the confrontation and let it be? In everyday life you can sometimes choose the latter course without any direct consequences. But in sport it has immediate consequences, destroying your self-confidence and self-respect.

Look at the following table and try to decide which points apply to you. Don't make heavy weather of it. The aim is to shed light on the various factors that can influence what happens on a football field. You can easily translate the examples given here to a different sport.

These rather unsubtle examples could be multiplied ad infinitum, but the point will be clear. On the football field, weaknesses that can either be concealed or that may have no immediate consequences in everyday life, are exposed mercilessly during a match and harm your game.

	FOOTBALL: for example, a match	LIFE: for example, a work meeting
Judgment	Can lead to anger/ frustration or to overestimating or underestimating your opponent; this will generally have an immediate adverse effect on your game.	You think your colleague is talking nonsense. You silently pass judgment, withdraw and keep your conclusions to yourself. There are no immediate consequences.
Unrealistic goals	Self-delusion becomes apparent within just a few minutes. When you try to give passes that are not in your suitcase, it leads to unnecessary mistakes, causing frustration.	You constantly get involved in a discussion you know nothing about. Colleagues remain polite and you leave the meeting feeling self-satisfied
Acceptance	If you are unable to reach a state of acceptance, for instance about your opponents' strength, the end result is frustration, which will have negative repercussions on your game.	A decision has been made that you don't accept (fewer mobile phone calls, for instance). You are very annoyed and decide inwardly to ignore it. You don't give a damn, and carry on as before.

Skills	You can't pretend to be fit or to have a good technique. If these qualities are not in your suitcase, it will immediately be obvious. The lack of these qualities will cause you to make mistakes or lead to exhaustion, resulting in frustration.	Someone without any leadership qualities can happily stay on as the chairman of the football club for twenty years.
Level of attention	If you have a short attention span, it will have immediate repercussions on your game; your actions will lack precision.	You spend the meeting reliving that great football match you played at the weekend. You occasionally nod to make it look as if you're listening.
Irritation	This will generally make you less focused, which will have immediate repercussions on your game.	Peter is going on and on as always, which really gets on your nerves. You switch off and decide to make a mental shopping list until he has stopped.
Discouragement	When you feel discouraged, you underperform. In desperation, you may start trying to give passes that you know perfectly well don't work. This will result in frequent loss of possession.	You notice that you can't understand a word of what is being said and announce that you have to leave for a dentist's appointment.
Fear	Fear is immediately obvious; you choke, you can hardly move your legs, you're cramp up, you lose speed. This is perfectly obvious to your teammates.	If you choose, you can hide your fear and it will have no immediate consequences for the meeting. At worst, your colleagues may notice sweat patches under your armpits.
Stubbornness	If your approach to the game doesn't work out and you keep on stubbornly applying it all the same, you are bound to underperform.	The subject of mobile phone use is on the agenda again. As a frequent caller, you always vote to allow private calls to be billed to the office. Next time your colleagues will take advantage of your absence and unanimously adopt a private calling ban.
Impatience	Impatience leads to ball loss immediately.	You keep looking at your watch to see if the meeting is finally over. This is unpleasant for your colleagues, but there are no immediate consequences.

Of course we are not suggesting here that a lack of skill may not lead to problems at work, or that a lack of attention may not cause trouble in your relationship. The point is that during a match, unlike everyday life, weaknesses are *immediately visible* and have immediate consequences. Remember that a lesson has not been learned until it has produced a change in behaviour. And that is less visible in everyday life than in sport.

You are probably starting to understand what people mean by 'coming up against yourself when competing', and what causes it. Moreover, it will now be clear why acceptance is always the first step towards progress. Remember that there is nowhere to hide during a football match, and that this is one of the most important causes underlying the sense of 'powerlessness' you may have there. The transition from unconsciously incompetent to consciously incompetent marks the beginning of all progress in your game. It is a prerequisite for self-knowledge, which every player must constantly recreate.

Is conscious incompetence the same thing as 'Good Mistakes'?

To grow, you have to make mistakes. Football consists of almost nothing else. Good Mistakes are mistakes that are made in spite of having the right intention. Once you realise that you are not yet capable of doing something and try to change that (conscious incompetence) the change will obviously be accompanied by more mistakes than you had been making before. If you discover that, as a central defender, you are not making any progress by playing the ball square all the time at your present level and want to change this into helping more to build from the backline, it is inevitable that things might not go right at first, especially during matches.

What does that look like in a match

The central defender, Peter, is given the assignment to build up from the backline more often. When he finds free space in front of him, he dribbles at least 25 yards and gives a diagonal pass to the right midfielder. This pass is just a bit too far away from the right midfielder, causing the ball to go outside the lines.

Peter the Story Thinker reacts like this:

'Oh no! There we go, it's happening to me again, thanks to my messing up we lose possession! And that, just before half-time with a 1-0 lead. Now the other team can keep attacking and maybe even equalise. If only I had chosen to play safe and played the square again.'

And this is how Peter the Action Thinker reacts:

'The dribbling up field went as planned, I gained a lot of distance, only my pass wasn't accurate. Next time, I'll take a better look at my teammate's position before giving the pass. And then it will definitely go better.'

You can see the pass going out of play as a 'good mistake'. The Story Thinker gets frustrated by it and that thinking will not benefit his game. The Action Thinker draws hope from dribbling up field, even though it ended with his pass going out of play. His non-judgmental way of perceiving will not adversely affect his game, but rather benefit it. By the way, it is also important to maintain neutral perception if the ball did reach the right midfielder exactly as planned. We don't mean by this that you cannot enjoy a beautiful dribble up field and an excellent pass, me mean remain calm and focused until the end of the match.

Let's revisit the reaction of the Story Thinker and the Action Thinker in the case that the ball does reach the right midfielder as planned.

This is how Peter the Story Thinker reacts:

'Yes! Fantastic dribble and what a stroke of luck that it worked and the pass was right on target! Nice just before half-time. This might give the opportunity to score another goal. I'm sure next time I'll be able to dribble up field and give a great pass so we create even more chances. I'm sure the coach will have noticed it too.'

The Story Thinker assesses his action in the first instant as lucky. Immediately afterwards, he becomes overconfident. Even more so, Peter is preoccupied with wondering if the coach saw his action or not and totally loses mental focus. This has nothing to do with being in the now and everything to do with the future.

Peter the Action Thinker reacts very differently:

'The dribble and pass went exactly as planned; the ball was passed perfectly to the right winger. Nice. Keep it up.'

The reaction of the Action Thinker is brief and will not lead to concentration loss or disruption of mental balance. Of course, no one learns overnight to apply this mental change, but as in so many cases the change is already initiated upon realising that two different approaches exist. Then the transition from 'unconscious incompetence' to 'conscious competence' and thus an important step in evolving one's self-awareness, has already been taken.

At this point we want to mention an exception to the rule of always keeping strictly to non-judgmental observation. It has to do with the advantage of 'trigger words'. At the risk of sowing confusion and introducing nuances that might seem to obscure rather than to clarify the issue, we feel this point must be mentioned here. A player can actually get a huge kick out of a wonderful individual action and will often play better because of it. The important thing is that a positive assessment does not upset the mental balance (as in the second example of Peter the Story Thinker), but of course that assessment can trigger enthusiasm that is beneficial to the self-confidence of the player. Expressions of this positive reinforcement (trigger words) we see all too often in matches of professional players. Common and appropriate trigger words are: 'tackle', 'positive' and 'keep running free'. Also making a fist after a nice action or exchanging a high five with a fellow player can also be good ways of boosting your morale.

Some players will outwardly show no sign of this positive reinforcement and express the trigger words only in silence. Enthusiasm about a successful action can 'excite' a player towards better performance. Each player must learn at what point to express her emotions and when it is wiser to hold them back. By consciously practising this during training sessions, the football player will 'feel' which reaction best suits her character.

PILLAR 6: ACCEPTANCE

Acceptance is the mother of all pillars. By applying the five pillars we've dealt with, you will learn that things you can't change must be accepted, and that this gives you space that allows for a faster recovery and faster progress. In Buddhism, this is often called 'As it is, not as you want it to be'. This means that both desire and disgust cause pain, and essentially reduce the space available for rest and a balanced mindset. Translated in simple terms into football: the desire to play differently than you're playing right now (in a match), the desire to win, and giving in to a sense of disgust about the results you've achieved, disrupt your balance and do not provide the necessary conditions to improve. The basic conditions for progress and improvement are acceptance and refocusing your attention on the quality of your actions.

The foundation of football is formed by calculating each player's unique playing style and forming the best strategy revolving around each player, her task and her position. Also taking into account the strengths and weaknesses of the opposing team. Each player has to recognise and take responsibility for her own task. If you stick to that task, then you can rely on each other and build a great team together. This commitment contributes to acceptance. For example, if you know you are going to build with three players and the right back is going to play higher up the pitch, the right winger can also run into the midfield space because he knows the right back will be playing higher up the pitch. This creates confidence. And if that goes well, you can build further as a team. Then if things unexpectedly go differently, you can accept it, because everyone did what was agreed upon.

As we pointed out when discussing the contrast between the consumer mentality and investing in your game, acceptance is an active attitude, as against complacency, which is passive. Acceptance increases your mental flexibility, whereas complacency restricts it. Acceptance brings calmness and self-confidence, complacency destroys your self-confidence. Complaining, protesting, giving up, all that produces unrest and noise. It leads to a rigid mental attitude. You've carried out the assignments to train Friendly Eyes and Good Mistakes, to increase your curiosity and self-knowledge, to set realistic goals, and to improve your self-discipline.

In the long term, these changes will translate into calm self-confidence, and therefore into an acceptance of the situation 'as it is, not as you want it to be'. This self-confidence will dispel tension and insecurity. Self-confidence means being convinced that you can perform to the best of your ability, not being convinced that you will win. Performing to the best of your ability means winning the match against yourself, not against the opponent (only half of the players can win a match, but in theory you can always win from yourself). This mindset gives you the opportunity of winning twice: from yourself, and if things go well, from your opponent too. What does it mean to 'win from yourself'? You win from yourself if you set yourself realistic goals in a match and strive to achieve them. You can learn to experience this as a victory.

Pillar 6: Acceptance during playing football

By using the previous five pillars, you have set some goals for yourself for the coming period. As you pursue these, there are bound to be setbacks. You may lose a match you expected to win, for instance, or sustain an injury during training. Make sure that you impress upon yourself that these losses, and even the occasional injury, are all part of the process. And that in spite of these setbacks, you are still on the right path. If you want to improve your awareness on this front and work on these goals, use the assignments from Intermezzo 3 and the *Mindset* Goals from Chapter 9.

Pillar 6: Acceptance in everyday life

You've just messed up an important assignment / lost an important match, and have the feeling that you could have done much better/won. That hurts, and you may feel unsure of yourself towards your superior/coach; basically, you hate the idea of discussing your 'failure'. When you catch sight of your superior/coach, you keep right out of his way. Stop trying to avoid this confrontation. Learn to accept that even losses are best talked about, and although evaluating a win may be more fun, discussing a loss can be more useful. So rise to the challenge and don't stick your head in the sand. There's no need to be ashamed, since you did what you could at the time. Listen to what your superior/coach has to say with an open mind, give your own opinion clearly, and write down what you consider to be the most important things to learn from the experience. Accepting disappointments instead of trying to forget about them will increase your insight and help you to make more rapid progress.

Acceptance

'If you accept your limitations, you can go beyond them.'

Brendan Francis

HOW TO DEAL WITH UNEXPECTED CHALLENGES

Is it unsportsmanlike behaviour if a football player consciously or unconsciously uses verbal and/or physical provocation to agitate the opponent and try and to entice them into story thinking and therefore into making mistakes? How do you best deal with (alleged) incorrect decisions and/or bias by the referee? Or being made to sit out the match for the umpteenth time by your coach?

Many players and goalkeepers of all levels try to influence the opponents and the referee to their own advantage. This seems to be totally accepted in the football world as it currently exists. This means that coaches, players, referees, spectators and parents need to decide for themselves how they are going to react to others and how they are going to behave themselves. We are not here to say 'this is right and this is wrong'. This Intermezzo goes beyond right and wrong and focuses on becoming an Action Thinker in all situations.

VERBAL AND PHYSICAL PROVOCATIONS

An explicit example of provocative behaviour in football, was during the World Cup Final penalty shoot-out between Argentina and France. Martinez, the Argentinian goalkeeper, purposely threw the ball away from the French players whilst they were walking towards the penalty spot. This forced the players to go and fetch the ball. Aurelian Tchouameni was clearly affected by Martinez's tactic and fired the 3rd penalty for France wide. The referee could have easily brandished a yellow card for the goalie's behaviour, but chose not to.

Before Kolo Muani took the 4th penalty, Martinez continued to try and throw the ball away, but this time the referee stopped him. Then Martinez immediately started shouting directly at Kolo Muani, just before he was about to take his shot. Only then did the referee give Martinez a yellow card. One could say that this 'broke the spell' of provocation as Kolo Muani stepped up to the spot and planted his penalty straight into the goal with conviction.

Martinez's antics might blur one's memory of extra time, when in the 123rd minute of the match, he made a heroic save. It was one of the greatest saves of all time denying the winning goal for France. One wonders if the antics that Martinez used to influence the French players in the penalty shoot-out were actually necessary? We will never know.

Another spectacular example of the way in which a world-class football player, who has consistently behaved as an Action Thinker throughout his career, lapsed into story thinking at 'le moment supreme'. This example is about the demise of Zinédine in the World Cup final between France and Italy. During extra time, with the score standing at 1-1, Zidane said contemptuously to the Italian defender Marco Materazzi, who kept pulling at his shirt, 'If you want my shirt so badly, you can have it after the match'. To which Materazzi replied, 'I'd rather have your sister'. This led to Zidane's notorious head butt, after which he was sent off the field. What exactly happened here? Both players lapsed into story thinking, and Zidane came off worst.

In most cases the provocation is subtler and the consequences less direct, although they may frequently be dramatic. Let's look at another example where we may encounter this behaviour in football.

At club level, it could be disruptive and undermining when an experienced player derogatorily says to a new young defender who managed to stop many forward attacks: 'I can't believe how well this youngster is playing, but I'm sure that when the pressure is on they'll crack.' These types of comments are mainly intended to put the other player off their game.

Bear in mind – recalling the example of Zinedine Zidane – that these verbal tactics also have repercussions for the person using them. The person who started this 'game' also runs the risk of lapsing into Story

Thinking and not being able to play at their best. There is no one answer to the question of whether these verbal tactics should be classified as right or wrong or whether they belong to a player's normal arsenal of weapons. Each player determines how they want to behave on the pitch. If you would rather go through life with a reputation for integrity and good sportsmanship, you won't choose this approach. If you feel that the ends always justify the means of winning a match, you might do so.

A Mindset football player would not choose this path, since situations of this kind do not even arise when you are in Action Thinking. We believe it's possible for players, referees and coaches to rise above the need to react. Each person can learn to be present in every match from their own internal strength, without being concerned how the other team, coach, referee or player is behaving. In the following assignments we will show you how to rise above and remain in Action Thinking. Chapters 5 and 6 will give you practical instruments in how to remain focused under pressure and switch the thinking mind off from external influences.

HOW TO DEAL WITH VERBAL AND PHYSICAL PROVOCATIONS

Team assignment: During matches of four against four within a small area, only one team gets an extra assignment from the coach, besides the tactical goals which both teams receive. The coach asks that team to purposely try to irritate and influence the opponents mentally. The other team do not know anything about this beforehand. **Attention**: do not overdo it!

For example:

1. Stalling when balls go outside the lines or throwing the ball far away from the player.
2. Verbal attacks on the opponent, e.g.: 'You're going to miss this, or 'Glad you're not that fast', or repeatedly calling them names or constantly making comments.
3. Physical intimidation, e.g.: regularly when the ball is nowhere near you, moving very close to the direct opponent and pushing her or grabbing hold of her shirt.

How can you best react to this?
Do not connect with your direct opponent by making eye contact, engaging in conversation or pushing back, but relax your body posture, take up space and focus your eyes on where you want them to be in order to adopt the right position. Use an instrument, for example inner music (Chapter 6) to allow yourself to focus on something uplifting rather than the opponent's attempt to distract you. If you notice that the behaviour of the other team is getting to you and the energy is seeping away from you and your team, no matter what, remain aware of Friendly Eyes. Even if a teammate constantly fails to make a good pass, react with Friendly Eyes towards them. For example, you give them a thumbs-up for a good attempt, you do not show a disappointed reaction, but you look towards them with an encouraging smile.

HOW TO DEAL WITH DECISIONS THAT WE PERCEIVE AS WRONG

Linesmen and referees of all levels make mistakes, for example when flagging offside. This does not mean that they are biased or unfair. It can happen that a linesman was just not in the right place and did not see the offside line at the right angle, or was surprised by a player stepping back. It is also possible that another player influenced their vision, or that they raised the flag because they expected it to be offside as it had happened like those three times before. Or they were in doubt and had to make a split-second decision.

These kinds of incorrect decisions occur regularly. We suspect that referees deliberately making wrong decisions are far less common than is generally thought. Realise that mistakes can be made to your disadvantage but also to your advantage. But still, many players and coaches have trouble with (in their eyes wrong) decisions.

INDIVIDUAL ASSIGNMENT

1. Accept that the decision has been made and there is nothing you do can change that.
2. Breathe deeply 3 times.

3. Relax your tongue and your shoulders.
4. Shake all of your muscles to get rid of any body tension.
5. Remind yourself of why you play football, use your trigger word.
6. Read Chapter 6 carefully for many practical exercises to bring you back into the here and now and away from the anger you are feeling that could wreck your game and affect your teammates negatively.
7. The chance of you getting a yellow-card if you follow these instructions is very low.

TEAM ASSIGNMENT

In a game form during training, the coach (functioning as referee) occasionally makes a deliberately wrong decision, e.g., the wrong team is given the throw-in, or a foul is given when it is clearly not the case. After the decision, the players immediately accept the referee's call and there is no verbal or physical reaction towards the referee. All involved immediately take up their desired position again. Now you have a real chance to practice for matches. Are you aware of your breathing, have you taken a deep breath, or is your breath high, fast and shallow? Is there any tension in your shoulders? Where is your visual focus? What is your trigger word?

How to deal with home whistlers (biased referees)

In the Netherlands the nickname 'home whistler' is given to a biased referee who consistently blows for their own home team. If a so-called home whistler is being unfair, it is wise that the coach (assistant or captain) speaks to them at half-time about their behaviour calmly, clearly and factually. This needs to be done without expecting any particular outcome and also with the insight that it serves no purpose getting into a long discussion or reacting emotionally. By naming the factual moments in the first half, the situation is brought to light. There is not a lot more that can be done at that moment. If in the second half the biased calling remains extreme, then after the match is concluded, you can choose to inform the board of your association/club. They then can decide whether or not to take the matter to the league or wherever these cases are looked at professionally. You have then done everything you can, accept that and have the insight to move on.

How to deal with your umpteenth time on the bench

If you have been put on the bench several times for the past few matches, when you believe that you had earned a place on the pitch, what on earth can you do? Most players get so upset that they eat themselves up from inside whilst pretending to be supportive of their teammates. They even begin to hate the coach and doubt every decision they make. Sometimes they start hating their teammates for 'taking their place'. Their joy for the game flies out the window and their motivation in practice sessions is at an all-time low. This also often affects the players life at home.

Assignment for when you have been put on the bench:

1. Accept the situation as it is and decide to dare to be curious.
2. Go to your coach and ask them when they might have time, at a convenient moment for them (not just before a match) to explain what you need to pay attention to for her/him to consider putting you in the game next time.
3. Ask open questions, e.g. 'What could I improve to have a better chance of getting more playing time? Exactly what actions are needed from me? I believe these actions are necessary... is that right?
4. Be curious and listen to what the coach has to say. Make sure you don't get defensive with 'buts'. Read the assignments in Chapter 3 about curiosity and open questioning. Acceptance and action are always the best way forward and will work in everyone's advantage. If you cannot accept the coach's answer, realise that it is better to look for another team.

What *'Mindset for football'* is all about is learning how to shut yourself off from any psychological games, and to remain relaxed and focus at the same time. Only by practising these situations will you become skilled in your reactions and be able to play freely no matter what is going on around you. Be courageous, ask your coach and teammates if they would be willing to do the exercises above. You will be astounded by their power and the results they bring.

Few are those who see with their own eyes and feel with their own hearts.

ALBERT EINSTEIN

CHAPTER 5

ACTION THINKING: THE ART OF CONCENTRATION

WHAT KIND OF CONCENTRATION DO WE NEED WHEN?

A concrete, simple explanation of what concentration really means, and of how players can train their own powers of concentration.

The level of concentration that Lionel Messi shows on the pitch is something that every player would want to achieve. He is a master of what the football world calls 'orientation', meaning being aware of the ball, the opponents, his teammates and the space in between, all at the same time. He sees everything around him and this allows him to make decisions at lightning speed. Another player who has world class concentration / orientation skills is Erling Haaland. Later in this Chapter, we will look scientifically and factually at how Haaland directs his visual focus to constantly achieve world level performances.

In this Chapter we are going to unravel the secret of how to train orientation. We will make focus tangible by splitting attention up into four concentration forms. It is possible to train each concentration form separately and then reconnect them so that they blend seamlessly into each other. By practising in this way your concentration will improve enormously.

So what prevents us from playing with Messi's and Haaland's attitude and training with their world class attention? Both lack of awareness and fear. Fear of losing, fear of certain actions, fear of trusting our skills. But especially the lack of awareness of how to train concentration. We all know the phenomenon of our thoughts 'racing like a crazy monkey'.

How wonderful it would be if we could calm these thoughts. With the right concentration you can teach the mosquitoes of Story Thinking to disappear into the background. In the following Chapters, there are clear exercises to train each of the four concentration forms specifically.

Concentration

To perform well in any sport, nothing matters more than concentration and in football specifically orientation. It is fundamentally necessary to find the right kind of concentration in every situation. Just as you improve your actions by practising technique, it is also possible to train the optimal concentration. Everyone knows that your game goes downhill immediately with even the smallest lapse of concentration. The result is blunders and sloppy mistakes. On the other hand, we also often hear references to players being 'over-concentrated'. We would argue that no such thing exists. Later on in this Chapter, it will become clear why 'over-concentration' is the wrong term: you can't concentrate too much, the point is that you might be concentrating on the wrong thing. If a player achieves the right kind of concentration in a match, you always hear the same kind of comments afterwards, which all have to do with *Action Thinking*: 'it all went automatically', 'I didn't have to think', 'I was totally absorbed in the moment (= the now)', 'I was completely immersed in the game', and so on. *Story Thinking* leads you away from where your attention ought to be, in the here and now. *Action Thinking* takes you to the point where all your attention is needed. When you have achieved perfect concentration, there are no distractions left to influence your game. You can learn to conjure up this concentration by practising it, again and again.

Many years ago the sports psychologist Robert Nideffer did some pioneering research in this field. The publication in 1976 of his book Attention Control Training was a milestone in research on attention control.

We have developed our own approach to concentration, which is partly inspired by Nideffer and also based on the newest scientific research of how the eyes of great players actually move during match play.

When it comes to concentration, the most crucial factor is learning how to control and guide your attention. Our method is based on four different types of concentration: scan and zoom are **external concentration**, your attention focuses on the outside world: your opponent, your teammates, the ball, and so on. This concentration is visual. Thought and feeling are **internal concentration**, your attention is focused on your 'inner world': thoughts, feelings and sensory experiences. This includes visualising an action, the tactics you have decided on with your team and your specific task, but also body awareness (breathing, muscle tension etc.).

Football players are constantly switching between the four categories of concentration: **feeling** (narrow-internal), **thought** (wide-internal), **zooming** (narrow-external) and **scanning** (wide-external).

Nideffer concentrations	Mindset concentrations
wide-internal	thought
narrow-internal	feeling
wide-external	scanning (visual)
narrow-external	zooming (visual)

Feeling: what do we mean by this form of concentration?

Let us clarify what we mean by feeling. Instead of constantly focusing on the way we feel and hoping that Story Thinking will finally disappear, we suggest stopping that and using tangible instruments instead to evoke the right feeling that will create clear thoughts. In earlier editions of *Mindset* we simply used the word 'feeling' as one of the four types of concentration. We heard from the athletes and people we train that they found 'feeling' a difficult and 'vague' concept. We now use 'feeling – use instruments' because the use of the instruments is tangible. The instruments describe what to do when you want to reach the concentration form that we earlier simply called 'feeling'. When too many thoughts are interfering with our visual perception (zoom and scan), we use 'the instruments' to clear our thoughts and evoke the feeling of action thinking. Applying 'the instruments' correctly changes our emotions and our body awareness. In other words using the instruments evokes the right feeling. You can conjure up physical awareness, for instance by moving lightly on your feet, and by listening to the sound of your feet. That is what we mean by body awareness or 'feeling', which bridges the gap between thought and observation. Without thinking, you will automatically create the emotions that shift you into action thinking, and escape from story thinking. These changes clear your thoughts and you will notice that they help you to feel strong both emotionally and physically.

Here are examples to clarify the four types of concentration

Someone looking at a group of horses standing in a meadow **scans** the whole area (**wide-external**). If he looks at the brush he is using to groom a horse, he **zooms** in (**narrow-external**). If he thinks of a clear plan for getting the horses into the stable efficiently, he allows his **thoughts** to range freely (**wide-internal**). From a familiar **feeling** (**narrow-internal**) he will make certain noises that always help to calm the horses and make it easy to move them. He uses the instrument sound to create this feeling.

How do you recognise the different kinds of concentration?

Perhaps it will help if you recall that you are constantly switching between scanning, zooming, thought and feeling all the time in everyday life. Take a situation in which you are cycling through town:

- You constantly have to pay attention to the road surface immediately ahead to check for direct obstacles or holes in the road and the objects very close to your bike (other cyclists, parked cars). That is **zooming**.
- You also have to pay attention to the traffic situation (is the next side road a one-way street? Is the traffic light up ahead red, is the parked car moving out?). That is **scanning**.
- Having looked well, both scanning and zooming, you decide to speed up, since the light is still green. That is strategy: **thought**.
- Then you let your muscles take over, you accelerate your leg action and enjoy the sensation of racing and of wind in your hair. This is body awareness, **feeling**.

How do you recognise the different types of concentration in football?
Imagine taking a corner in a match situation:

- You walk towards the corner flag. You choose to look exclusively at the flag, nothing else; This is **zooming**.
- Then you shift your attention, you look specifically at the position of the goalie, your teammates and the opponents in and outside of the penalty area. This is **scanning**.
- After looking carefully, both by scanning and zooming, you decide exactly in which direction you will kick the ball. (Your thoughts are brief, not to be confused with visualisation). This is strategy: **thoughts**.
- Then you let your muscles do the work, they are supple and loose, you breathe slowly and deeply, your jaw muscles are relaxed, your tongue is relaxed, you see the trajectory of the ball in front of you (spin, curve, speed, height, where does the ball touch your foot - visualisation), you walk to the ball and kick it full of confidence. This is body awareness, **feeling**.

Is it possible for a player to consciously train concentration and to train shifting attention from one category to another?

It is not only possible to train concentration, it is fun and easy. Four simple exercises to clarify these differences. If you do these exercises, you will immediately feel what is meant by each of the different categories. They are exercises in the four different categories of concentration. By doing these exercises you are training your mindset.

The following exercises can be adapted to all sporting disciplines or other situations in everyday life. What exactly are you focusing on?

Exercise 1: Zoom

Repeat this for three minutes: use your eyes **to zoom only on the ball** and the contact moment of your foot on the ball. Let nothing else enter your vision at all, look solely at the ball and the foot at contact, this demands a high level of concentration. Now constantly gently kick the ball back and forth from standing still to 1 ½ feet distance. Keep tapping the ball 1 ½ feet further with your foot and then put your foot on top of the ball to stop it and notice explicitly the following:

1. Touch moment: where exactly does your foot touch the ball when you gently tap it forwards - see the moment of contact and see the spot your foot touches the ball.
2. The ball in motion: how exactly does the ball spin on the ground after the tap - what is the speed, the direction, the contact with the ground, the pattern of the movement of the ball?
3. Stop moment: where exactly does your foot come in contact with the ball when you stop it? Each time in the same place? Or does it change? Do you see anything new?

Note! Be aware of every little deviation of your eyes! When they are not tracking the ball at the correct moment or not paying attention to where your foot touches the ball at the moment of impact, this is incorrect concentration.

This seems like a very simple exercise that you may have done already a thousand times. Be aware that it is these exercises that Olympic football players do in their training and which they keep repeating to constantly improve their concentration. Only if you are 100% committed and curious about keeping your eyes on the ball and being aware of the moment your foot contacts the ball, are you really training your concentration. Are you genuinely aware that you are only working on zooming, or are you having all kinds of thoughts and letting your eyes take in way more than just the ball or your foot? *If you have those thoughts, or let your eyes wander, realise you are not zooming. Use Friendly Eyes, and start again!*

Exercise 2: Scan

Agree with your coach and teammates during a practice match to concentrate **exclusively on scanning** for five minutes. This means that you purposely let zooming go and are only paying visual attention to where your teammates are, the opponents and the space around you. You will all be surprised how much mental energy that takes. Zooming in on the ball becomes secondary, so do tactics. It is extremely important that you let go of the result to be able to practise pure scanning.

1. Where does your direct opponent stand in relation to you?
2. Where does the best reachable teammate stand in relation to you?

3. Where are you in relation to your line, do you see where the openings are and to whom you can pass the ball?
4. What is the position of your goalkeeper and that of the opponent?

By using your attention only to scan the pitch and the position of all players, you will become aware of what that brings. You will be able to perceive earlier and more clearly what is taking place over the whole pitch. Note: this is an exercise and may come at the expense of receiving the ball well, because you are not concentrating on zooming. This is how you can train concentration consciously and specifically.

Exercise 3: Feeling

By now we hope it is clear what 'feeling' is. A deeper exploration follows in Chapter 6, where we explain the importance of body awareness through the use of Instruments. For four minutes, practise keeping your concentration exclusively on feeling.

First minute: Be aware of the tension in your jaw during all the actions. Is your jaw tense or loose, does tension increase when doing certain actions? While running, when you kick the ball, when you intercept the ball, head, pass? Concentrate constantly on relaxing your jaw. Tip: if you find it hard to feel if your jaw is loose, soften your tongue and your jaw muscles will automatically soften too.

Second minute: How do your shoulders feel during all actions? Runs, passes, tackles? Do your shoulders tighten more during certain actions? If so, let your shoulders drop and feel your shoulder muscles loosening up.

Third minute: Now focus on how the muscle tension in your legs feel. When you are receiving a ball, when you pass a ball, when you are running, when you tackle? What do you notice?

Fourth minute: How do your forehead and facial muscles feel? Is there ever a frown in your forehead? If so, when and why? Softly make a correction and relax your facial muscles.

Bring structure into training concentration

If world class players struggle with concentration, it cannot be any different than that you also struggle with this. It is important to become aware of the constant, unnecessary tension in our bodies. In order to learn to let go of this tension you will have to train with a clear structure. How do you do this? With persistence and discipline, perform the above exercise for feeling, coupled with pillar 3, curiosity and the world of concentration and awareness will open up to you. You will learn how to relax under pressure and have much less tension. This in turn will free up extra energy so that you can play at your highest ability throughout the whole match. This will motivate you to train concentration consciously. It is simple and challenging at the same time!

Exercise 4: Thought
You have already been training the concentration form 'thought' by using the six pillars and working on the assignments. As explained earlier, without Action Thinking (a balanced, present mind) a player is not capable of making clear and efficient tactical decisions.

Another excellent exercise for match practice
Focus your attention exclusively on Friendly Eyes and Good Mistakes for yourself and your teammates for the whole match. Every second, every moment, from start to finish. You persist no matter what blunder you make or they make. Don't be preoccupied with tactics, only with an intention of kindness and forgiveness. This may sound incredibly soft, it isn't. Jackie's experience with multiple Olympic teams, professional tennis players and world class performers in the music world too, makes it clear that it is very challenging even for the world's highest-level performers to think in this fashion, as much as they would love to. We subconsciously believe that being hard on ourselves and others, especially under pressure, is necessary to make progress and win. It is perfectly normal to shout 'Idiot, why did you do that?' in a punitive inner voice, indeed, it is actually expected of you, that is the indoctrination of a traditional mindset. Saying to yourself: 'You are giving your all and the others are doing their best too, it's ok, we're going to play the next ball well, we are doing great' is a much less used approach. Actually, quite mad when you think about it more deeply!

By doing this kind of exercise regularly, it will become more and more an automatic approach and will support switching between the other concentration forms from a deeper, quicker subconscious level. This process will lead to greater self-confidence and in turn also to better results and more enjoyment.

As you can see in the diagram on the next pages, the four forms of concentration and Instruments (Chapter 6) can have both a positive and negative side. Do you use the concentration of a Story Thinker or of an Action Thinker?

What causes inaccurate and sloppy play?

The diagrams, scanning and zooming are related to how the eyes observe (visual). This means that you know exactly when to use your eyes to follow the ball, that you see where your teammates are in the field and that you also see where your opponents are positioned and where the opening in the field is. It's about being fully aware of the space around you and the opportunities it offers.

This focus has to do with your observation of the outside world. By far the most important kind of concentration in football is the ability to switch from zooming to scanning and vice versa. If you stay fixated on one or the other for too long, this will immediately cause inaccurate actions or not positioning well. That is because your timing will no longer be right because of poorer anticipation, as a result of which you have a lapse of concentration and you do not receive or deliver the ball properly. Poor switching can also cause you to be 'out of position' or not well positioned in the free space. Often scanning and zooming are disturbed by thought. By becoming aware of this you will be able to train these two concentrations and notice immediate improvement.

Where do things go wrong, and why?

The most common mistake is switching immediately from thought to visual concentration, without using the necessary 'bridge' of feeling (body awareness).

STORY THINKING

FEELING

1. Negative
2. Uncertain
3. Giving up
4. Impatient
5. Hesitant
6. Listless
7. Stubborn
8. Fearful
9. Predictable
10. Dependent
11. Distracted

INSTRUMENTS

1. Negative trigger-words
2. Haunting images
3. Rushed / irregular breath
4. Paralysed
5. Restless
6. Rushed or no rituals
7. Distracted eyes
8. Distracting sounds
9. Noise in your head

THOUGHT

- Focusing on the past and future
- Judgmental
- Too many thoughts
- Irrational

SCAN

Distracted by:

- Spectators
- Weather conditions (dislike)
- Anything moving around the pitch (other than the ball and players)
- Coach's and opposing team's attitude (arrogant, cheeky, irritating)
- Referee and linesman

ZOOM

Distracted by:

- The direct opponent
- Irritating/arrogant/physical
- Opponent's facial expression: unfriendly, aggressive
- Facial expression & body language teammates; unfriendly, discouraging, drooping shoulders,
- Clothes, ball (away games) and football boots
- Coach/parents/spectators/ referee and linesmen; comments, shouting

WHAT DO YOU C

ACTION THINKING

FEELING

1. Positive
2. Self-confident
3. Perseverant
4. Patient
5. With conviction
6. Motivated
7. Flexible
8. Courageous
9. Creative
10. Autonomous
11. Focused

SCAN

Focused on:

- Spectators (encouragement)
- Weather conditions (accept)
- Position of direct opponents, teammates and line
- Seeing spaces and passing possibilities
- Position of goalkeeper
- Adapting position to changes in game situation
- Pitch (surface/speed)

INSTRUMENTS

1. Trigger words
2. Visualisation
3. Breathing
4. Muscle tension
5. Recovery
6. Rituals
7. Eye control
8. Sound
9. Music

ZOOM

Focused on:

- Ball; direction/flight/height/impact moment
- Opponent: preferred leg, dummy, foot position
- Opponent coming at you: speed, which leg in front
- Coach/ parents/ teammates for encouragement
- Opponent's body language; physical and emotional state

THOUGHT

- Present
- Observing without judgment
- Tactics: short and clear

NCENTRATE ON?

Many players direct 'scan and zoom' from 'thought'. Feeling is skipped. This directing is incorrect because *thoughts* are conscious and the action must take place on the subconscious/automatic level. This is possible only if *thoughts* go to scanning and *zooming* via *feeling.*

Here is another example of how the four forms of concentration can be used. Players sometimes linger in thought for too long after losing possession of the ball. For example, a player switches their thoughts to tactics and says 'I must keep switching quickly and get back into the required position.' In itself, that can be a valid thought, but not if they move from this thought immediately to scanning and zooming, because then there is a much greater chance of too much tension remaining in the body. It is also detrimental if the player remains stuck in tactical thoughts and keeps repeating them internally; then the thoughts change into constant noise and belong to Story Thinking. The correct way is: after a short tactical thought, use the concentration form feeling (the Instruments) - be aware of your breath, keep your jaw and muscles loose and then switch immediately to the visual concentration of, scanning and zooming.

The concentration required for optimal action or positional play cannot be directly driven from preoccupation with long thoughts about tactics. In the following diagram you can see examples of how the concentration forms work during a match.

	Zoom	Scan	Feeling	Thought
Action Thinking	Correct estimation of the passing allowing you to intercept the ball	Passing the ball to your teammate who is free	Muscle tension; loosening of shoulders and legs, deep inhalation and exhalation and eyes on the ball in preparation when taking a direct free kick	Having confidence that the tactics given to you by the coach are clear, very occasionally letting them come to mind, then immediately reconnecting to feeling
Story Thinking	Incorrect assessment of the passing action of the opponent causing you to act too early and get easily passed (attention was not focused on the ball but on the upper body of the opponent)	You pass the ball to a fellow player but did not see that an opponent could intercept	Constantly looking around you, High rapid breathing and very tense shoulders and legs muscles when taking a direct free kick	Constantly being busy with all kinds of irrelevant things. Having frequent thoughts of what is not going well with you and your teammates instead of focusing on the tactics that were discussed beforehand

What is anticipation and how can I improve it?

Anticipation consists of scanning and zooming which both form and drive orientation. So without actually using the word 'anticipation', we have already written a great deal about it.

Anticipation is actually much easier than the average player thinks; many people assume that it is a really tricky skill to acquire. It is very rare for specific training sessions to be devoted to it. In fact anticipation really just means 'looking specifically and carefully'. Remind yourself constantly to look with your eyes, don't think about things, focus on eyes and feeling your body. This is the way you can learn to anticipate better. By doing the concentration exercises in this Chapter with your whole team, you can be assured that both your anticipation and that of your teammates will improve by leaps and bounds.

A documentary on Lionel Messi shows **the physical** difference between him and the rest of the players. His head and eyes almost never stop moving. Left, right, in front, behind, where are the opponents, where are the goalies, who is free, where is the ball, how can I run free? You can only do this if you are in the now of Action Thinking. When your head is full of thoughts, you will forget to scan and zoom. The concentration form feeling (loose muscles, breathing through etc.) will be almost completely lost and that is the reason why most players regularly fail to anticipate properly. To improve your anticipation, you need to be aware of what you are looking at, what exactly are you scanning and zooming? The upper body, the free space, the opponent's foot, the ball, where your fellow players are standing, where the body weight is of the players around you, both teammates, the opposing team and the goalies. It's a lot!

Scanning and zooming on the pitch, the hard facts

Haaland's eyes

As we mentioned earlier, Norway's Erling Haaland is an exceptional striker. He is 6 feet 3 inches tall and both strong and fast. He scores an exceptionally high number of goals. What makes him so unique?

Norwegian Geir Jordet has an explanation for Haaland's rarely seen figures. 'Football is a game of information gathering. Haaland is a machine in that,' he reveals in an interview.

Jordet, a professor at the School of Sports Science in Oslo, has been researching psychology in football for over 20 years and is specialised in 'scanning'.

'Scanning is looking away from the ball, prior to the moment a player receives the ball,' Jordet says. He watched and studied huge amounts of match material, close-up footage of 120 footballers from the English Premier League. In doing so, he counted when a player 'scanned' his surroundings on the pitch.

'It was abundantly clear that the more players scanned, the better they performed. The most frequent scanners were Frank Lampard and Steven Gerrard.'

Jordet expanded his research method over the years, now using eye-tracking, and criss-crossed Europe to conduct research in the Premier League, the Bundesliga and Ajax's youth academy, among others. The football world is following his studies with increasing interest.

How do you measure 'scanning'?

'It's quite simple,' says Professor Geir Jordet. 'And anyone can do it at home. You do have to look at one player and not the ball. You will see that all the top players are scanning.' Then it's simply down to counting. 'If a player looks away from the ball, that's one scan. If he looks away again, that's two.' Jordet and his researchers look at the number of 'scans' of a player in the 10 seconds before he receives the ball. 'If a player scans five times in those 10 seconds, he has a scanning frequency of 0.5.'

Many of the world's best attackers have been studied, but the intensity of Haaland's scanning Jordet has never seen before.

Jordet says: 'It is a great pleasure to see him scanning. He uses it to find space, to get into good scoring position and to see where the ball will end up in the penalty area.'

That indicates extreme awareness of his surroundings on the pitch. It provides Haaland with a striking statistic. 'He is almost never offside. Very rare for a player who lives on the edge of offside.'

Jordet continues: 'It is intuition, his perception of space, to actively look for where his teammates and opponents are standing and then receive the ball. When the ball comes to him, Haaland looks away again to see where and from which angle the defenders are coming to pressure him.' **(scan)**

That gives the striker the opportunity to take the ball directly into space in the approach, away from the approaching man-to-man defender. Eye to eye with the goalkeeper, the Norwegian then remains icily cool. 'Then you see him actively looking at the goal, the goalkeeper's position and an opening to aim at.'

The frequency at which Haaland looks around is exceptionally high for an attacker. 'We have studied him several times and he is always between 0.35 and 0.50 scans per second,' says Jordet.

Haaland looks away from the ball every two to three seconds before receiving it **(scan/zoom/scan/zoom)**. 'The average scan rate of other Premier League attackers is between 0.27 and 0.28,' says Jordet. 'Haaland is a machine, collecting information very effectively.'

'In a stack of DVDs with 120 players,' Jordet recalls about the information he collected 15 years ago, 'there were also 40 strikers. All top strikers, you will remember all their names. But only one of those players was above 0.28, figures somewhat comparable to Haaland's now. That was Dennis Bergkamp.'

Timing of Frenkie de Jong

Jordet also mentions Frenkie de Jong, a professional Dutch football player. 'I'm a big Frenkie fan! An excellent scanner. He executes effortlessly and elegantly. And his timing. That's essential. Scanning at the right time.' Every time the ball is played, a footballer should look at the ball **(zoom)**, according to Jordet. 'So that in between ball contacts, there is no need to follow the ball, because you already know where it is going. That's the moment when you have to scan.'

'Actually quite logical, right? This is exactly how players scan at top level. Asked whether you can also train scanning, Jordet replied: 'We can observe it, analyse it and give feedback. This also makes it easier for players to train on it.'

Science can help if your ego can handle it

Our first *Mindset* book 'a mental guide for sport' was written in 2008, based on Jackie's observations of professional and recreational tennis players over a period of 25 years. In those days we didn't have eye tracking to be able to factually prove exactly what the eyes are doing. What we did have was our own experience, seeing literally, that players thought they knew where their eyes were, but actually didn't. By recording the players on video and then showing them a close up of their eyes (the old-fashioned way) it was possible to show the players that they weren't paying attention to what they thought they were paying attention to and that they were easily distracted. These observations were the start of the *Mindset* books. Science is now helping players to understand this even better as mentioned above in *'Haaland's eyes'*. Unfortunately, the ego can still sometimes get in the way of learning and there remains a lot of denial when it comes to taking responsibility for your own concentration. Players of all sports will often say or think; 'But I was paying attention'. This happens because it is confrontational to admit to yourself that you might not have been paying as much attention as you thought you were. The ego plays funny games with us and sometimes gets in the way. Lack of curiosity and self-knowledge can be the real challenge. Keep using

Friendly Eyes to bring yourself back to the right visual concentration and have no judgment if you forget to pay attention to the correct cues. That you recognise it is already great progress and with effort you will get better.

Where should my concentration be during a free kick, corner or penalty?

This is the right order for concentration, not only for football, but for all sports and up to No. 4 also for everyday life!

1. look towards your goal **(brief scan)**;
2. choose your goal **(brief thought)**;
3. visualise your goal **(feeling)**;
4. check your breath, shake your muscles loose **(feeling)**;
5. focus briefly on the ball until your foot touches it and keep following it **(zoom)**

After the action, immediately switch from zoom back to feeling and then back to scan and zoom, thoughts can be left behind, your eyes will not cheat you.

Where should my concentration be during half-time?

When you go to work, you decide on a plan for what you will do that day. The same applies to football. Before the game, the team knows what the game plan is and everyone is given their own task.

At half-time, the coach will adjust the game plan (thoughts) if necessary. Because that situation is in many ways no different from a situation at your work, we call this 'at the office'. This is the only place where it is wise to stay in thought for longer than about five seconds without falling into Story Thinking. By this, we mean that clear tactical reflection and discussion are essential. But it is imperative that your own thoughts do not take on a life of their own.

Half-time = at the office

What happens to concentration at half-time? You can compare this period with being 'at the office' and in a brainstorm session with colleagues about the next exciting project at work. This is where 'thoughts' from

Action Thinking play an important role. Let us show you what we mean with the points listed below.

1. Always make sure you can sit comfortably during half-time. The break is for listening, thinking and drinking! **Thoughts**
2. Hydrate immediately, wipe off your sweat and sit alertly but relaxed. Drink enough, as it has been scientifically proven that fluid loss leads to significant loss of concentration. **Feeling**
3. Focus on regulating your breathing. **Feeling**
4. Only when you notice that your body is relaxed, start to reflect on how you played, what you did well and what you want to improve. **Thoughts**
5. Listen carefully to the coach and your teammates. Listen to every word and whilst looking at them, still remain aware of your breathing an the tension in your muscles. **Thoughts and feelings**
6. Before you go back onto the pitch, close your eyes and visualise the tactic. See yourself playing with joy and energy. **Feeling**
7. Say briefly, possibly out loud, a trigger word to bring yourself into the right energy. **Feeling**

How can you correct the wrong kind of concentration?

If you find yourself in the frustrating and noisy, confusing concentration of Story Thinking (as described in the chart on page 118), there is only one way to change it: switch to the positive concentration of Action Thinking. *The Action Thinking chart corrects the Story Thinking chart.* Of course we are well aware how difficult and complex this may be at times. The mosquitoes often keep imposing themselves because they are a part of our personalities. Still, it is easier than you think. Let's look at four examples illustrating how you can apply a specific correction to the wrong kind of concentration:

1. **Scan:** If you are distracted by the spectators, or the coach of the other team, focus your attention on the position of your teammates and your opponent.
2. **Zoom:** If you are intimidated by your opponent's appearance (for instance because they are tall and strong), change your focus to their upper body to help you anticipate where the ball will land.

3. **Feeling:** If fear is making it impossible for you to relax and play freely, become aware of your muscle tension, shake your muscles, lower your breathing and use a trigger-word to bring you back into the now.
4. **Thought:** If you are distracted by negative thoughts, switch immediately to Friendly Eyes, linked to a realistic self-image; as for tactics: base them only on the visual, and not on all the thoughts in your head. When you do this, you will immediately shift to Action Thinking.

What is the ideal kind of concentration?

When a player is in a flow ('in the zone'), their concentration is purely visual (external) and they constantly switch back and forth between scanning and zooming. This happens automatically. The more easily a player can switch between scanning and zooming, the better their concentration is. Only in the spaces between actions is it wise to shift their concentration to short thoughts or feeling (both internal concentrations). Here a quote from the tennis world explaining exactly how flow works followed by a moment that Chloe Kelly describes when scoring the winning goal in the European Championship final against Germany.

Monica Seles, who was ranked number 1 in the world for 178 weeks in a row and won nine grand slam tournaments, once made a very insightful comment in an interview. She said that she was constantly in the zone when playing her best tennis, but that '*once you think about being in the zone, you are immediately out of it*'.

That means that you can only get into the zone if your concentration is in the visual, and that you switch in between actions from feeling (using the Instruments) and not from thought. The demands of tactics and technique are met *automatically*. As soon as your concentration shifts to judgmental and/or future thoughts ('Oh, I'm playing so fantastically now, I hope I can keep it up'), you lose the flow, because you slip back into story thinking.

Chloe Kelly in an interview with Jonathan Ross, was asked if she relived the moment of the winning goal. She answered, 'Yes, I watch it every day! But honestly every time I watch everything changes, and the noise of the crowd, **for me at that moment it was silent,** but every time I watch it the roar of the crowd gives me goose bumps still today.'

Chloe's goal and reaction are clearly of someone in the flow. She says 'everything was silent'. But in reality, the crowd were going mad, it was a corner situation, she was surrounded by defenders, it was the 110th minute of extra time, yet for her it was silent.

Often in a pressure situation, at all levels, a player will constantly be thinking, 'we've got to score, we've got to make this, if we don't score now, we'll lose.' Chloe remained in the now, at the first opportunity from the corner, right in front of the goal, she just didn't quite manage to get her foot on the ball. But she remained calm and managed to tip the winning goal in with a toe punt after it rebounded off the goalie. Any thoughts such as 'I can't believe I missed that chance' would have immediately interfered with her instinctive reaction. And even though, after the game, she called it 'her worst goal ever' it brought the European Championship home to England.

The non-concept of 'over-concentration'

Now let's return to the non-concept of 'over-concentration', which we mentioned at the beginning of this Chapter. All four categories of attention have to be deployed at the right time. If you linger in one of them for too long, your concentration will lapse. That does not mean that you are 'over-concentrated', but that you have not switched in time to the correct focus. As soon as you become aware of this, you will no longer have to struggle with the confusing and nonsensical concept of 'over-concentration', but will see that you have simply stayed focused on the wrong thing for too long.

ASSIGNMENTS TO IMPROVE CONCENTRATION

1. When you start a training session or match, decide to always consciously walk onto the pitch from the right concentration, namely from 'feeling' and not from the traditional way 'thoughts'. Do this by using the exercises described in this Chapter. Be aware of your breathing, shake your muscles loose, make sure you have a gentle smile on your face. Listen to all the sounds around you. Don't identify with your 'thoughts', focus all your attention on feeling and then switch to visual attention, scan and zoom.

2. Discuss with your coach and teammates whether it is possible to work separately on all four different forms of concentration.

3. Use the 'Where is your concentration' chart in this Chapter to answer the following questions:
   (a) Which of the four concentration forms have you mastered best from Action Thinking? Thoughts, feelings, zooming or scanning?
   (b) Which of the four forms of concentration have you mastered least from Story Thinking?

4. After answering question 3, decide which of the four forms of concentration you could best work on to get into Action Thinking:

i. Thoughts
ii. Feeling
iii. Zoom
iv. Scanning

Be clear and specific about what you want to improve regarding your concentration. Write it down and look at it every time before you go to a training or match.

Let it be clear, this training never stops! Olympic athletes are working on this day and night and if you understand how to train, it is a joy. You will definitely see constant improvement. However, it is important to maintain a realistic self-image. Just consider how long it takes to make technical changes.

Go to the online concentration course 'Discover' and watch videos showing exactly how to train and play matches from 'feeling instead of thought.

www.friendlyeyes.com/discover

Imagination is more important than knowledge. Knowledge is limited. Imagination encircles the world.

ALBERT EINSTEIN

CHAPTER 6

STORY THINKING: HOW DO YOU ESCAPE FROM IT?

USE THE INSTRUMENTS TO ACHIEVE THE RIGHT FEELING

The practical application to be able to play every match with self-confidence and clear focus. The magic key to achieving these goals is emotional balance. At the start of every action, the football player must use the concentration form 'feeling'. There are nine Instruments to help you find that feeling.

In Chapter 1 we wrote that everyone can achieve the following things:

- To play freely during a match situation instead of tensing up.
- Not to have to fight against yourself during a match.
- To feel acceptance and self-confidence instead of frustration.
- Not to feel irritated by your teammates, your coach, the referee and the other team.
- To gain insight into your talents and limitations.
- To transform your fear of failure into faith in yourself.
- Knowing how to focus/concentrate, both during training and in matches.
- Not to be influenced by the score.
- Not to feel pressure from anyone watching the match.
- To change the 'battlefield' feeling into a 'playing field' feeling.

The following Instruments will help bring you into the concentration form *feeling*. Before the action commences your body awareness must be optimal. Thoughts will diminish and the malfunctioning machine of Story Thinking will be conquered by the presence of mind of Action Thinking.

The nine Instruments

1. Trigger words
2. Visualisation
3. Breathing
4. Muscle tension
5. Recovery
6. Rituals
7. Eye control
8. Sound
9. Inner music

> We want to repeat that you can't achieve the right kind of concentration if you switch directly from thoughts and/or negative feelings to zooming and scanning. This is the most important mistake made by players at every level. When your emotions take control of your game, you can turn this around by using the Instruments listed above to balance your mind. You use these Instruments and the six pillars to neutralise your emotions and bring you in the feeling of Action Thinking. The chart below represents the differences in concentration between the two mindsets. On the left-hand side, you see that thought in Story Thinking takes up a big part of your minds energy. This leaves less space for scanning, zooming and feeling. On the right-hand side you see that in Action Thinking, scanning and zooming get more space because feeling is more emphasised, not thought. In this way thoughts of Action Thinking are short, clear and tactical.

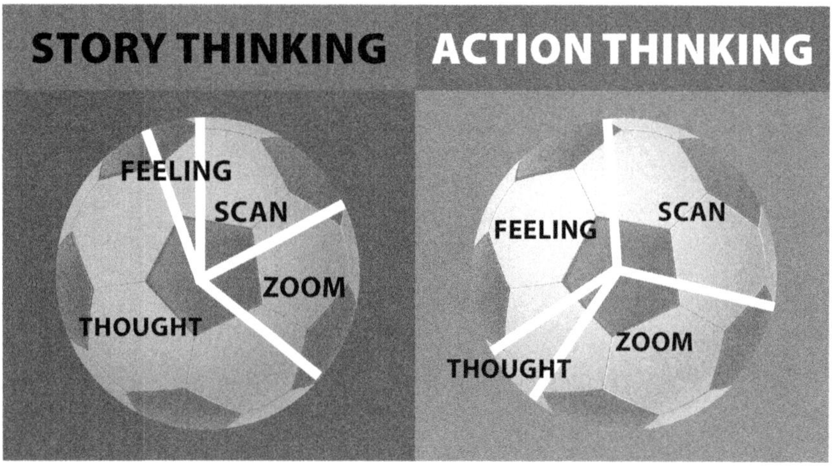

In the following pages, we present a systematic approach that can help you eliminate frustration, anger, tension, the fear of failure and a sense of helplessness during a match and to break through your old patterns. Players often 'know' that these are important issues, and yet fail to deal with them because they have not really come to grips with them and they have remained purely theoretical ideas. What is more, 'rational' thinking often wins over intuition. You know that you must change, you even know how... but you can't bring yourself to do it (you are controlled by Story Thinking). So what is the formula for breaking this impasse and reaching an attitude that reflects the 'light side' of action thinking? The answer is simple: by training MENTAL skills. Focus your attention specifically on training the four concentrations, the six pillars and the nine Instruments, as often as technique or tactics. It is not complicated; the method is consistently simple, tangible and practical.

THE NINE INSTRUMENTS

1. Trigger words

What are trigger words?

Trigger words are one or two words that you repeat to produce a positive influence on your actions. Many football players like to write them down, so as to be constantly reminded of them. Others prefer to say them, either silently or out loud. And some even opt for a tattoo to be reminded of it always!

Trigger words and 'priming'

The social psychologist John Bargh made a study of 'automaticity', the ability to perform a task without your mind having to concern itself with all sorts of minor details that are involved in that task. Other psychologists had called this mental process 'mindless', but Bargh claimed that the processes involved were not mindless but unconscious or 'automatic'.

An interesting part of his research was a study of 'priming', in which subjects in one group were required to perform a task after being given a lot of terms associated with elderly people such as 'old', 'grey' or 'forgetful'. The other group was not 'primed' with these words. After this task, the subjects were asked to go to a different room. The astonishing thing was that the first group displayed signs of old age: they walked noticeably more slowly than the other group.

If you give one group of players an assignment and add terms of encouragement ('you will certainly be able to do this'), and give another group the same assignment with a more discouraging message ('this is something that everyone finds really difficult'), the first group will adopt a different attitude and will learn the task more quickly and satisfactorily. The idea behind 'priming' is that you can influence behaviour by the words you use. And this explains how trigger words can be used in football. Trigger words influence behaviour far more effectively than long-winded instructions, because they set in motion automatic, unconscious processes. By doing so, they prevent you from slipping into Story Thinking. When Merel van Dongen, now an experienced Dutch international and player for Atlético Madrid, was 16 years old, she trained at the Hogeschool van Amsterdam, under the guidance of coach Hesterine de Reus. This was in 2012, well before the time when women's football had reached the world stage. The training programme was set up to give young players the chance to train full-time, alongside their school or studies. It was the first time the football players had left home. Hesterine had the progressive insight to also integrate a mental training programme and asked Jackie to work with her, the staff and the players. Thus, a nine-year collaboration with the young professional players was born. Merel trained for three years with the *Mindset* method from the age of 16 to 19 years old. Jackie and Merel kept in touch and when the online courses were created, Jackie asked Merel if she could share what she had learned over those years. This was now 12 years after her formative mental training.

Merel was happy to share her knowledge: 'Before every match I literally write Friendly Eyes on my wrist. Because it helps me to focus on what is important and perform at the highest level with a sense of enjoyment and self-acceptance.'

She went on to say: 'I think it would help everyone in the world. It doesn't matter where you are or what you are doing, it helps you to love yourself and be proud of yourself. And at the same time, it encourages you to get the best and strongest out of yourself, to really become that person in the future who you want to become. That's what Friendly Eyes means to me. It gives you a lot of pleasure and at the same time you are never done. It is developing yourself, with fun and happiness.'

The trigger words *Friendly Eyes* have been used by Merel almost daily for 12 years. You can really call this *priming*! Of course, her talent, commitment and perseverance are indispensable. What is special about this story is that she has additionally applied the same willingness and work ethic towards the mental side of the game. By constantly reminding herself what matters, both on and off the pitch, she has had a wonderful and balanced football career.

Trigger words and Story Thinking

Negative 'self-talk' undermines self-confidence and leads to frustration. It is the most visible example of the negative effects of Story Thinking. But what about positive self-talk? You might think that this too is a kind of Story Thinking. It is true that positive self-talk consisting of a lengthy discourse doesn't work at all. It may even get you stuck into Story Thinking. 'Wow, I made a really brilliant tackle and my last pass was perfect: a few more actions like that and I am sure that I will be selected again!' That belongs in the category of Story Thinking and is not helpful.

Positive self-talk should consist of short exclamations – what we call 'trigger words'. The emphasis is on what you do want to achieve (your goals) and not on what you don't want to do. A clear instruction that leads to positive physical action. Short words that can immediately be translated into action. 'Not so fast!' or 'Don't do that!' are meaningless and seldom have any effect. Useful trigger words are 'Look for the tackle', 'I can do it', 'I'm fast and strong', 'Scan the whole field', 'Zoom on the ball' or 'Friendly Eyes'. It may also be useful to say 'It's o.k.' or 'Good mistake' after an unsuccessful pass, because it prevents negative emotions cropping up. If you miss a pass as a result of a terrific action by your opponent, accept it and move on. Acknowledging great play by your opponent gives you space and releases pressure. It ensures that you will carry on with a positive mindset. You don't have to look up to the opponent, but appreciating beautiful play, is part of an 'Action Thinker's mindset' in football.

Fists, notes and mantras

Trigger words are a way of keeping yourself alert. They introduce a kind of structured courage into your game. You could also say that by saying something intentionally out loud, you trigger the subconscious. Before every match, Merel van Dongen (Dutch International) writes 'FE' and 'GM' on her wristband. These letters stand for the trigger words 'Friendly Eyes' and 'Good Mistakes'.

The way that works best for you will depend on your personality. By practising different trigger words, you will find out which ones suit you best. Don't expect miracles, hard work is always the key to success, but working hard does not mean you cannot enjoy yourself. Use trigger words to remind yourself that you are playing for fun and because you love the game of football!

Never underestimate the power of words. It is interesting to compare trigger words to mantras. Mantras are words or expressions that are repeated constantly during a certain form of meditation. It is used to transport the person concerned into the here and now. This form of meditation can help you to stop identifying with the emotions and thoughts of the past and future, making attention less likely to drift. In our terms, we might say that mantras help to banish Story Thinking and heighten alertness. And that is what mantras and trigger words have in common: they transport you to the here and now and enhance your presence of mind.

2. Visualisation

Visualisation is the link between the mental and the physical. It is the best manner to overcome fear, to accept it and cope with it. You learn to face fear, greet it as a known friend and replace it with the feeling that you would prefer to have under pressure. That's why it is so important. Visualising means conjuring up pictures of situations and of the way in which you will respond and act in those situations. It is thinking in images. Professional athletes often visualise their actions beforehand.

The players, including Merel van Dongen, who attended the three-year *Mindset* course in Amsterdam, were trained in this. In a survey of Olympic coaches and international athletes in a wide range of sports, the respondents were asked to identify the most important element of their

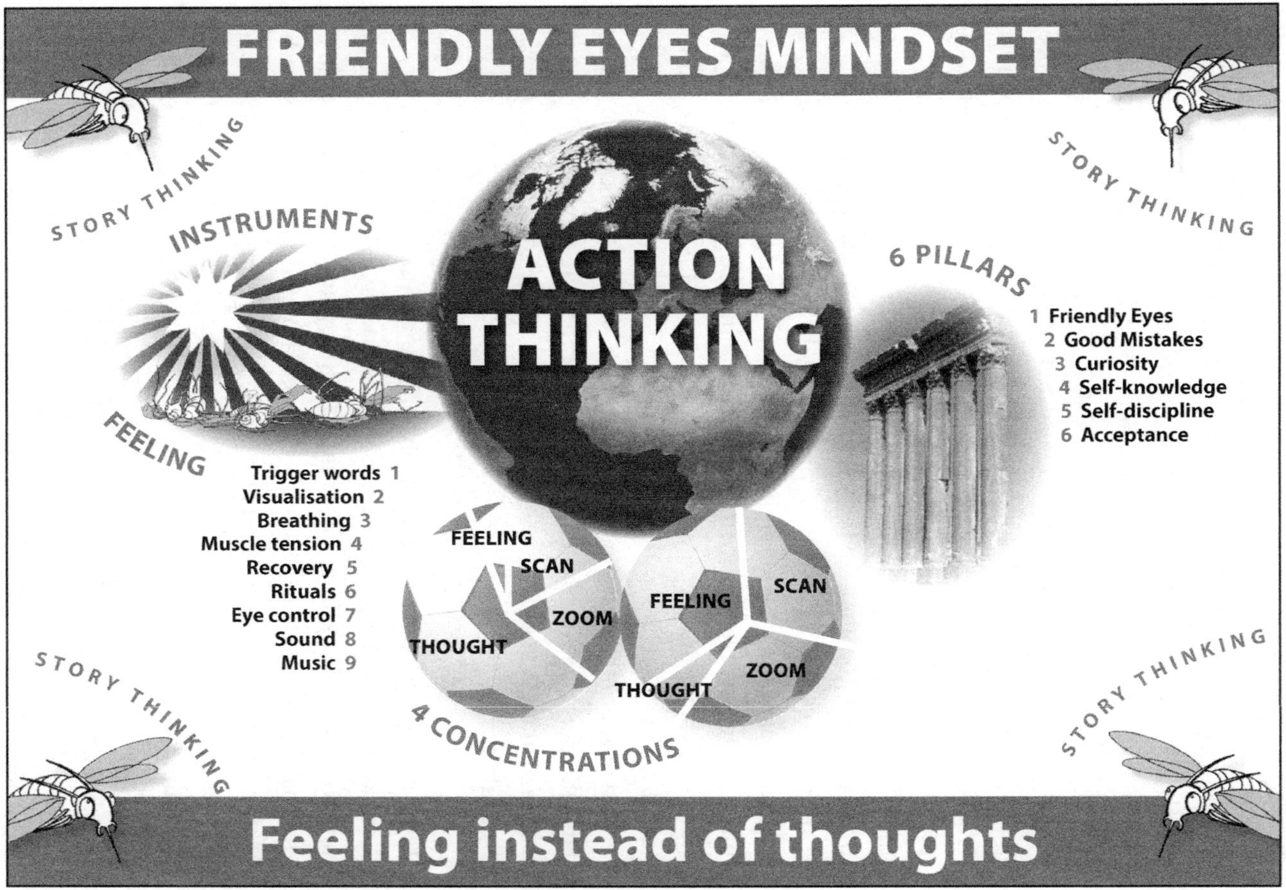
FRIENDLY EYES MINDSET
STORY THINKING
STORY THINKING
INSTRUMENTS
ACTION THINKING
6 PILLARS
1 Friendly Eyes
2 Good Mistakes
3 Curiosity
4 Self-knowledge
5 Self-discipline
6 Acceptance
FEELING
Trigger words 1
Visualisation 2
Breathing 3
Muscle tension 4
Recovery 5
Rituals 6
Eye control 7
Sound 8
Music 9
FEELING
SCAN
ZOOM
THOUGHT
FEELING
SCAN
ZOOM
THOUGHT
4 CONCENTRATIONS
STORY THINKING
STORY THINKING
Feeling instead of thoughts

mental training programmes. Without exception, 'visualisation' came at the top of the list. One popular slogan is: You have to see it, to be it.

Visualisation extends beyond the football game itself, you can practise it daily. A necessary part of visualisation that athletes often forget involves visualising the emotions that arise during the game. The best way to learn to deal with match tension is by evoking the emotions that a match can bring. If you deliberately conjure up fears, they become familiar to you and you learn to recognise them more quickly. You practice replacing those emotions with desirable ones. As a result, you will be able to recognise fear arising, accept it and with a lot of experience and training, switch to the presence of mind of Action Thinking. By now it is clear that the tools to switch to feeling are much more powerful and many times more important than the fearful images of Story Thinking.

Be sure to visualise instead of verbalising. Don't allow Story Thinking to take possession of you: you don't need to fight it off, that will only make matters worse. Just turn your attention inward and picture exactly what you want you are going to do on the pitch. Just doing this will in itself help you to relax.

Visualisation allows you to shift you into Action Thinking. It stimulates the part of your brain that controls automatic processes – the opposite of analytical processes – and wards off the syndrome of 'paralysis by analysis'.

You know more about visualisation than you think

A situation that everyone in the world recognises and that directly relates to visualisation is cycling. Yes cycling! When you get on your bike to a destination you cycle to less often, but which you do know, you search your mind for landmarks. You don't make a long story of this, you know 'Oh yes, at that supermarket I turn right and then later at the government building I can take the short cut and then past Miriam's house on the left. That's the quickest way to get there.' Yes, you can visualise. You do it much more often than you think. It's time you apply it consciously!

Everyone who likes football enjoys watching matches on the television. How does it actually affect you? The next time you go to practice or play a match, you suddenly notice a difference in your game: everything is going more 'automatically'.

Apparently, the images have done something to your body. Even the most inexperienced of players have discovered that visualisation can have a tangible impact on their game. You see yourself playing just like your heroes in yesterday's final. By watching the world's best players in action, you form a picture of the various skills and attitudes. The way they carry themselves, their persistence, how they pass, tackle, run, head. Becoming a master of visualisation will help you 'beyond words'!

In what situations is visualisation easy to apply?
At corners, tackles, dribbles, penalties, half-time, injury time, sitting on the bench, it doesn't stop! It's better to ask: What situations can't I use visualisation for? The answer is: there are none. Many players say: 'But I have no idea how to do it.' Our answer is: 'Have you ever practised visualisation purposefully?' With the right effort and with perseverance, everyone can do it. To test this, go and do the following exercise before you step onto the field. You will surprise yourself!

Practising visualisation
When visualising for the first time, it is wise to lie on your back, on a mat, your bed or the sofa, with your eyes closed and your hands on your belly, to start. The appeal of visualisation is that when you start getting used to it, you can even do it at home, at the office, on the beach, while cooking or on a walk.

Engage senses
Try to see the action you are visualising in front of you. It helps to use several senses to facilitate visualisation. For example, hearing - hear how your foot hits the ball, how your breathing sounds when you sprint across the pitch, the referee's whistle, the sounds that your teammates make. Or the aromas and touches: the smell of the grass, the trees in the distance or the feel of your clothes against your body.

Visualisation exercise 1 at a training session - a point of improvement
1. Make sure you lie comfortably on your back (with your hands on your stomach), close your eyes and regulate your breathing so that it is

slow and deep. Breathe ten times deeply in and out. You will feel your hands rising and falling with the in and out breath filling your lungs up softly.

2. Now go to a crystal-clear moment in a training in which you are striving to improve. It might be how you approach a tackle, a technical skill or a game situation that has been frustrating you and you would like to lift this part of your game to the next level.
3. Deliberately awaken those helpless emotions. See how you normally lose the plot, get angry, want to practise something else, become impatient and see how that affects your playing skills.
4. Feel your breathing start to falter a little because you are annoyed that the situation is happening again.
5. Immediately call a halt to your annoyance by using kindness and change your faltering breathing into deep calm breathing.
6. See yourself reacting differently in the same practice situation, also see an improved result in your game. Enjoy in your mind how well things are going. Let yourself play the perfect ball, perform the perfect tackle. *Pay attention! Often at moments like this, players say: 'Yes but I can't play at that level, I'll never manage that' or they start comparing themselves to teammates.* Start from your own strengths, don't get discouraged, because that is only Story Thinking playing games with the mind. Go back to Action Thinking and SEE yourself performing the perfect action and how nice it is to be able to do that.
7. Finish by saying to yourself: 'I can do this, I am doing well, I am going to give everything to play my best football and be satisfied with myself.'

Visualisation exercise 2 when training - a strong point

1. Make sure you lie comfortably on your back (with your hands on your stomach), close your eyes and regulate your breathing so that it is slow and deep. Breathe ten times deeply in and out. You will feel your hands rising and falling with the in and out breath filling your lungs up softly.
2. Now go to a specific part in a training that you know you are very skilled at.
3. Recollect images of yourself using that strong skill of yours. Let the emotions associated with it consciously come to you. See and feel how much energy and pleasure that brings.

4. Feel your breathing flow through smoothly through your whole body. Feel the satisfaction of this skill you have mastered and imagine how you can create new situations that will enable you to utilise this skill even more frequently.
5. See the new images of these situations in which you didn't previously realise you could apply your skill to them and enjoy every new discovery you make. If a smile appears on your face that's normal, because this is fun!
6. Conclude by saying to yourself: 'I see how strong I am and that I have a real skill that I can use in many different and unique situations. At every training and match I will use this talent.'

Visualisation exercise 3 - a match

1. Make sure you lie comfortably on your back (with your hands on your stomach), close your eyes and regulate your breathing so that it is slow and deep. Breathe ten times deeply in and out. You will feel your hands rising and falling with the in and out breath filling your lungs up softly.
2. Now start looking at all the preparations you take care of before a match. See yourself putting on your match tenue. See how you tie your laces, put on your shin pads. See how you look in the mirror to make sure your hair is right. You see a woman who is strong and ready for a match.
3. You see yourself walking onto the pitch, with a firm stride, your shoulders back, your breathing calm and regular, your muscles are loose and you have a relaxed and focused facial expression. You are ready.
4. You might feel some anxiety; you're used to that and know it's normal and welcome it as a friend. You shake your muscles even looser, you use your trigger words 'I'm ready, I'm strong' and you breathe deeply. You look at your teammates and it feels familiar. You see the opposing players and let all the emotions pass you by. Without them there is no match. You know that you are ready and well prepared.
5. You listen to the coach and the captain; you take your position on the pitch and you see that there is nothing to fear and that you are able to persevere the whole match. You go through different actions and

positions in your mind. You feel strong while running across the pitch, you feel strong during every tackle, you enjoy the physical challenge.

6. You see yourself breathing deeply when there is room for it. At an injury time out, or just before a corner or free kick. *When visualising, you always go to feeling rather than thoughts.*
7. You let several different scores pass through your mind, but you don't attach any value to them. 1-0, 0-1, 1-1. You always visualise being there, until the last moment, with total strength and commitment to give your all. The score has no influence on your effort. You see that a figure cannot control you. You are the master of yourself.
8. You finish the game, sometimes with a win, sometimes a draw and occasionally with a loss. You see yourself giving a hand to your opponents, to your teammates and you are satisfied, because you gave everything.
9. You walk off the pitch with confidence and self-respect and look forward to receiving feedback from the coach and your teammates.

You can practice the above visualisations on your own. If you do so with focused attention, fear, frustration and anger are guaranteed to have much less of a grip on you during matches. After all, you've seen it all before and you've dealt with it.

Visualisation is a skill that should be practiced every day from Action Thinking. You can do it for a few minutes, do it whilst sitting in the train, car, whilst you are cooking or having breakfast. Even on a bicycle - pay attention, of course - but it's all possible and well worth the effort.

3. Breathing

Breathing is the most important factor when it comes to regulating match tension. Breathing exercises (or Pranayama) have been at the heart of Eastern methods of meditation for thousands of years. Pranayama is a Sanskrit word made up of the words for control (yama) and life force (prana), and embraces a range of breathing exercises that help you to banish tension from your body and to achieve a tranquil state of mind. Its techniques empty your mind of thoughts and calm the ego.

Irregularity of the breath is the first sign of Story Thinking. This has to be seen separately from the normal physical effort involved in football.

The quicker a player becomes aware of irregularities in their breathing, the quicker they realise that Story Thinking is looming.

As soon as you focus your attention on breathing, you step out of Story Thinking and automatically shift to the here and now of Action Thinking. Past and future disappear, and you are in direct contact with your body. Focusing on breathing is key to most forms of meditation: the flow of thoughts and emotions is interrupted, with the objective of attaining 'full presence'. In Buddhism, this state is referred to as 'pure awareness' or 'selflessness'. In a football match, focusing attention on your breathing will help to boost your concentration to the maximum.

There are well-known techniques to calm your mind and get your emotions under control. It is striking that in the world of football these techniques are hardly used at half-time, if at all. We know from experience that becoming aware and regulating your breathing makes an important contribution to reducing tension during matches.

Awareness of the role of breathing during practice situations and games

As soon as there is any room during a match or training, it is extremely important to bring your breathing deeper and lower. Players often react to this comment as follows; *'You don't understand, I'm totally exhausted, of course my breathing is shallow.'* It goes without saying that after long periods of action, a player might run out of breath. What is forgotten is that there are also many moments when a player does have the opportunity and time to consciously breathe deeper, as long as they are aware of the timing of this.

Moments when breathing can very easily be brought deliberately lower and deeper are before corners, injury time outs, direct or indirect free kicks. But there are so many other moments. If you have just made a long pass, then you know you have a few seconds in which you can take a longer, deeper breath. You might think: 'what does that matter?' It matters a lot, as you will notice that you will be much less tired than usual if you manage to recognise these recovery moments. When you become proficient at this, you will also find that you have less muscle pain the next day. Because by breathing through, instead of (unconsciously) holding your breath or breathing shallowly, your muscles receive much more blood flow, they can function better and recover faster.

Breathing exercise to reduce tension before the game and at half-time

A technique that works well during half-time is the 'echo exhalation': after you have exhaled, you hold your breath for a moment and then exhale even further out, so that the last residue left in your lungs also disappears. This quickly brings you into a state of deeper recovery. You cannot apply this technique while playing, but you can do it during half-time or when waiting to play.

- Inhale deeply through your nose;
- Expand your belly when breathing in; this way you know you are breathing deeply;
- Exhale long, hold your breath for a moment and exhale again, until all the air is out of your lungs.
- Repeat 5 times and experience the immediate peace of mind

This technique helps to break down the lactic acids in your body, provide your brain with sufficient oxygen and makes it easier to focus on the now. You come into the right concentration (feeling) and you learn how to let your nerves go and let match tension flow away.

Research on breathing and decisions

Research has shown that people make better decisions when breathing in between six to nine times per minute. Realise that if you do the above exercise at half-time, you will be better able to hear and reflect on the coach's tactical instructions and also those of your teammates. On top of that you will walk onto the pitch in the second half as an Action Thinker.

4. Muscle tension

How often do our legs and arms feel like lead when we come under pressure? It is imperative to know how to be relaxed and focused at the same time when regulating muscle tension. Most football players don't pay enough attention to how their muscles feel during matches, whether they are tensed up or loose. Recognising this requires conscious training. During matches you often see that football players move with little confidence; they let their heads and shoulders droop and hang. It is known that even at international level, due to fear and competitive tension, players restrict themselves from playing at their best level. They have the feeling that they are completely 'exhausted' or unable to sprint at full speed. This happens especially when players fall into Story Thinking. Then it is almost impossible to transmit a task from thought to your body. To conquer this, it is imperative to frequently shake all your muscles loose and feel that you are capable of much more than you think. This is because players often want to 'command and force' themselves to move faster and tackle harder, rather than allow themselves to move faster and tackle wisely. Directing yourself with 'Friendly Eyes' and with encouragement will always work better than putting yourself under great pressure and release muscle tension, especially when you purposely shake your muscles loose at every possible moment. Moving from the right muscle tension brings you to the right energy level to be able to achieve and maintain good concentration. This becomes automatic when you train it daily.

Exercise to recognise muscle tension

1. During a training, consciously hunch your shoulders and put your leg muscles under pressure so that they feel tight.
2. Hold onto this feeling for three minutes.
3. Feel what this kind of muscle tension does to your energy.
4. Now shake your muscles completely loose, gently jump up and down, shake your hands loose, let your shoulders relax completely, and shake your legs one by one.
5. Now perform exactly the same exercise for three minutes, but this time from constant conscious relaxation. Note that obviously you need muscle tension to play football well and accurately, but you will feel yourself how much is needed and how much is too much!
6. After those three minutes, check how you feel. You will notice a world of difference in the energy levels you feel when hunching and tight vs flowing and loose.

Now realise that in matches, due to tension, you often play without even realising it, like in the first three minutes of this practice. No wonder you are often broken at the end of the first half!

By repeating this exercise regularly, you will be able to save so much energy during training and matches. Story Thinking will be a ghost of the past and Action Thinking will be unconsciously taking over at all moments.

5. Recovery

Without a good understanding of what recovery is and how it works, you will find that much of the match passes you by. Making conscious use of recovery time is crucial to being totally focused at the start of each new action. This is of an invaluable importance and has been discussed at length previously under 'visualisation' and 'breathing'.

Usually, after tense moments or even after a hard-fought action, players continue immediately to the next action - sometimes of course this is necessary, depending on what happens on the pitch, but sometimes this happens purely as a result of panic and also anger at losing possession.

How often does it happen that after making a brilliant move, you then immediately make a huge blunder? This can often occur because you have not taken enough recovery time to get into the right feeling, although you could have done so had you been more aware of the game situation. There are almost always two or three seconds when you can shake your muscles loose and breathe deeper.

Exercise for recovery moment

1. At your next training session, pick one moment you wouldn't have noticed otherwise, in which you have three seconds to breathe deeper and shake your muscles loose.
2. At the following training, choose two such moments.
3. When you are aware of this and have become skilled at choosing the right recovery moments - without compromising your game - resolve, at any time you can in a match, to lower your breathing and shake your muscles loose.

The coach's role in helping their team recover well is of great importance. Sarina Wiegman speaks of 'a virtual fireplace for down time'. The fireplace was used to create an atmosphere where players could relax and feel comfortable enough to share stories and get connected with each other. She helps the players realise that it's important to get the job done, but just as important to take time to switch off. Guiding players to become aware that when you work hard, it's really intense, and everyone needs to be totally focused which costs energy. She says, 'The demands are really high, so you also need to have some time to switch off, do other things and clear your head.'

Learning how to recover well is not only important during a match or training situation, but also extends to the whole process of coaching and training on and off the pitch.

6. Rituals

Rituals transport you to the 'now' and create a sense of security. They are the final step towards producing the right feeling for the beginning of play. That is why they are so important and should not be underestimated. You could qualify them as dynamic meditation. Rituals are fixed patterns of behaviour before and during matches, used to achieve the right kind of concentration and relaxation.

Alex Morgan, a US international, says of her preparation for a match: 'I always put my right sock on before my left sock, take a little nap and eat the same food before a match. Right before the game I put on my headphones and do visualisation, imagining myself in the match.'

When we read such a statement in a blog, or we watch a video on YouTube or an interview in which a player like Alex describes it, we often think, 'oh, interesting' and it stops there. For anyone who wants to make mental progress, it is not only necessary to visualise but also to perform conscious actions that constantly bring you back into the moment itself.

By focusing your attention on your right sock first and then switching to your left sock, you avoid Story Thinking. Your attention is focused and it feels familiar.

Power naps and eating rituals

A well-known phenomenon among professional players is having a power nap before the match. For some players this is a necessary ritual. Instead of fighting nerves, they learn to relax their bodies and trust to rely on the restorative power of sleep. A power nap of 10 to 20 minutes will suffice.

Preparing your food perfectly is a ritual that is often forgotten. What time do you plan your meal before your training or competition? What are you eating exactly? What effect does it have on your energy? You can change these things into set rituals that work in your favour. Talk to a professional nutritionist about this if it is not yet part of your team's programme. You will be astounded at how important it is to understand the power of nutrition.

Feeling safe through conscious choices

Rituals are known to give you a sense of security. They are anchor points that provide security because they are always the same. Well-known rituals are: rearranging an item of clothing (pulling at your shirt or shorts), touching your hair, touching your nose or eyebrow, tying your laces in a certain fashion, listening to music before the game, and so much more. They are a means to bring you into the now, the mindset of an Action Thinker. If a player gets out of balance, rituals can help her to regain her balance and rhythm. Most players have all kinds of rituals, but they are not aware of them. They have developed these rituals over time, during the many training hours. It is useful to consider whether they are useful rituals, do they bring you into the now, or are they 'habits' that just happened? Rituals are not 'just something'. They are actions that you perform consciously, so that they can be used - after practising them – 'unconsciously'. It is important to repeat your rituals constantly and always in the same way (that's what they are rituals for!). Rituals thus become an unconscious action that take you away from Story Thinking and into Action Thinking. The trigger word 'Friendly Eyes' that Merel van Dongen writes on her wrist before every match, in this way has become her go to ritual.

Exercise for rituals

1. Before every training session and match, pack your football bag in exactly the same way. For example: your towel is folded in a certain way and put into your bag first. Your food is in a plastic box and includes nuts and fruit. You folded your two pairs of socks along with your two hair ties and put them next to your towel. You have clothes with you for showering after the training/match. You have shampoo and cream in that familiar fancy toiletry bag of yours. You have your notebook with your trigger words with you. A pen in the side pouch that you can

immediately grab for when there is something said that you can learn from and don't want to forget.

2. Play your favourite music prior to training and competition. Choose the playlist that perfectly prepares you to perform at your best. Experiment with different songs and experience what effect they have on your feelings.

7. Eye control

Eye control is an awareness of where you focus your attention. As you know, eye control is a specific awareness of whether you are scanning or zooming. We have written about this extensively in Chapter 5. It is important to recognise that sometimes you keep your eyes focused on something for too long or feel drawn to something or someone because Story Thinking has you in its grip. To keep your perception optimal, it is imperative to be aware of what your eyes are focusing on. This prevents being influenced by unnecessary external stimuli. This is an indispensable tool for getting into Action Thinking.

A player needs to learn and become aware of what her eyes are paying attention to exactly. Are you easily distracted or annoyed by the behaviour of your fellow player(s) or opponent and do you stare at them? Are you looking at airplanes and the like? Then eye control is essential! What are you doing with your eyes between actions? Do you regularly look at your coach, your parents, your teammates? Are you aware of this? We sometimes cannot help but stare at something we find scary or annoying. Our eyes seem to get hooked on where emotions are leading us. By noticing exactly where your eyes focus, a new world can open up for you. Ex-Dutch international and goalkeeper Sari van Veenendaal always used to juggle three balls in the dressing room before the match. She says she does this to make sure she is focusing on what she chooses to do. It is a ritual based on eye control and leads you away from thoughts to feeling. Max Verstappen, Formula one world champion racing driver, also juggles three balls before performances. We hope that it is becoming clear that all world class performers have routines that bring them into feeling instead of thought.

Eye control awareness exercises

1. Before training: do an exercise to awaken your eyes. One of the simplest exercises involves keeping your eyes focused for three minutes only on a still football ball, your shoelaces or an inspirational quote in your notebook.
2. During the coach's explanation: do you see what is happening around you, do you stare at the ground, or do you only look at the coach or also all of your teammates? What is the most useful way to observe? Keep your eyes mainly on the coach, but also be sure to watch the reaction of your fellow players. This is how you learn to be fully present and understand the dynamics of groups energy and how different people react to the coach's explanation.
3. During training, when an exercise is finished: be determined to be aware of what your eyes are focusing on until the next exercise starts. You'll be surprised how often you let your eyes wander to completely unimportant things. Like: who is watching us, what is that gentleman over there doing at the end of the pitch? Why is the dustbin upside down, can't anybody else see that? And so on. By being aware of this you will conserve a lot of mental energy. Just rest your eyes softly on a space in front of you or far into the distance, that way you make sure that you are not being distracted.

Finally, in training or competition, be aware that you IMMEDIATELY need eye control when the following occurs!

You are playing against 'that opponent', 'THAT opponent' you know! Or you are dealing with 'that referee'. You can't help but stare at them all the time. They are so 'annoying/strong/irritating/beautiful/unsportsmanlike/ugly/terrifying and so on. The moment they step onto the pitch, your eyes get inexplicably caught up with their energy and you can't stop looking at them. Face this and restore your focus with a friendly smile that recognises what Story Thinking can do with your focus when you are unaware of the Instrument 'eye control'.

8. Sound

Another excellent way to redirect attention from your thoughts is the use of the instrument sound, which will help you shift immediately into Action Thinking. The sounds we refer to here are coming from the outside. Concentrate on the sound your foot makes when kicking the ball, the sound of the ball rolling over the ground. The sound of the ball when the other players kick it. And in between also focus on the sound of your own breathing. This will help to prevent you from being distracted by external, irrelevant noises as well as helping you shift from thought to observation and feeling. By focusing on sound, you use your senses to move away from Story Thinking.

Exercise for sound

This is one of the most beautiful ways to practise feeling.

1. Go to a blind wall or a ball catcher.
2. Practise the following kicking techniques:
   (a) Instep, drive/kick
   (b) Inside of the foot
   (c) Outside of the foot, flick kick
   (d) Point of the foot, toe punt (be careful)
3. Concentrate fully on the sound, as if you put a listening horn against your ear and hear how each individual step produces a different sound.

Realise that you are actually listening to your own symphony. You are making music together with the ball. You know which note is right and which is slightly off. No judgment, stick to sound and make technical progress from feeling rather than thought.

Competition exercise

If in a match you find that fear is starting to paralyse you, the sound of your own feet can bring you back to body awareness and free up your body to start moving loosely again.

This is a perfect example of how to use the concentration form feeling instead of thought. Sound is sensory, not rational.

9. Music

Music will help you to concentrate and keep Story Thinking at bay, we see that everywhere now, on the bus, the train, the plane, even at home on the sofa. Before training sessions and matches it is an excellent way to get into performance mode.

Leah Williamsom, England's Captain, was asked, 'What kind of music did you play before the final?' Leah explained that she had the role of preparing the music. 'I did the music throughout the tournament, pre-match on the bus and in the changing rooms. So (before the final against Germany) I just let the music do the talking. (…) No need to hype people up and get them too over excited. Strip it all away, we've given our lives to get to this moment, why would we not enjoy it? (…) I played Mamma Mia from ABBA.'

The importance of music is so clear in this example, and how important it is to recognise that these moments that you have worked so hard for, need to be enjoyed! Music will help you remember that.

We want to go even deeper than music from your favourite playlist. We propose that you can use 'inner' music during a match. Inner music can help you move away from the judgmental and critical voice in your head. It can also serve as a way to find rhythm and balance. Music can calm you down and relax you, or quite the opposite, revitalise you and give you more energy.

During a match, inner music can be used to help you to escape from the clutches of Story Thinking.

The right song immediately brings you back into the feeling of Action Thinking. Many players don't understand how music can play a role during a match. But we think readers can quickly understand by drawing from their own life experience. Think of a party: whether or not you can get into the right mood may well depend on the music that is being played there. Bear in mind that music can help you to evoke whatever atmosphere you want on the pitch, whenever you want. So realise that music can have a powerful influence on your mood. It can galvanise you or calm you down; it is a magic potion that is used far too little.

Exercise for inner music

1. Choose for yourself two very different songs that you listen to before the start of training. One is an uplifting, powerful song and the other is a mellow, chilled song. For ten training sessions you alternate listening to one song or the other. After the training, write down what effect the song had on how you felt going onto the pitch. After ten evaluations, you will notice which song has what effect on you. You use this knowledge to decide which song you will use on the field, in your mind.

2. Now you have discovered which song does what for you. For example, that one relaxes you and that the other whips you up. You start playing that song in your head for one minute whilst moving around the pitch.
3. When you completely lose your way in a match, call up the song that puts you in the right feeling. If you are low on energy, choose the uplifting song. Are you fired up and angry? Choose the calming song. This will always work better than getting caught up in anger, frustration or lack of motivation. Another great way to play from feeling instead of thought.

Having explained and discussed a variety of Instruments that can help you move away from Story Thinking, we want to review a few of the points from the Action Thinking chart in Chapter 3. We have taken these abstract points and shown how they relate to practical, tangible elements in football. By using Instruments to bring about a change of concentration: beginning each action from feeling instead of thought.

Action Thinking	Feeling = use instruments
now	rituals
relaxed	recovery time / breathing
presence	sound / muscle tension
alert	trigger words / eye control
realistic self-image	game plan corresponding to skills
self-development	short and long-term mental targets
calm	breathing
confidence	visualisation / trigger words
unconscious	breathing / music
being	rituals/ breathing / focus on action instead of the score / trying to perform as well as possible instead of winning

ASSIGNMENTS FOR INSTRUMENTS

To improve your concentration and to start each point with the right feeling, it is important to gain an understanding of how to use the Instruments that have been described. Be aware of the fact that you can practice all of the Instruments in everyday life. You do not need to be in a training situation or a match.

1. Trigger words
2. Visualisation
3. Breathing
4. Muscle tension (flowing movability)
5. Recovery
6. Rituals
7. Eye control
8. Sounds
9. Inner music

1. a) Which of the nine Instruments do you use most efficiently during a match?
   b) What benefit do you derive from it in terms of concentration?

2. a) Which of the nine Instruments do you use least?
   b) Can you explain why?

3. a) Which of the nine Instruments do you feel you neglect and which ones could you use more often?
   b) How are you going to apply that in practice?

4. For the next 4 weeks, make a conscious decision to use at least one new instrument. Use your new Instrument first during practice matches and training sessions. Pay attention to the effect that this has on your concentration. Work on it until it becomes automatic, and then use it to your advantage in match situations.

IMPROVE YOUR FOOTBALL SKILLS FROM FEELING INSTEAD OF THOUGHT

THE BEST APPROACH TO TRAINING TECHNICAL ASPECTS OF YOUR GAME

One of the biggest mistakes that players make is trying to improve their technical football skills from sheer willpower. They are convinced that they can only improve their technique through hard work. Of course, to realise your full potential it is necessary to make the greatest physical effort, although to make technical improvements and changes in your game, this is not the right approach in the initial phase.

It is necessary to realise that if you try to make a technical change only from 'forcing' and 'pushing', you are exhausting yourself without feeling what is going on. When you train with this approach, it will be almost impossible to effectively bring changes to your technique. This is one of the reasons why football players sometimes get despondent when they focus on technical pursuits, due to their inefficient initial approach to bringing about change.

With the small specific technical adjustments needed to develop a better tackle, dribble, header or pass, constantly putting yourself under pressure is counterproductive. You need space and time to notice the small nuances and feel what is needed to make the technical improvement you are striving for.

A brilliant way to practise: but he was made out to be a fool

Here is a fabulous and factual example from the world of tennis, which will then be translated to football. Richard Williams, the father of the sisters Venus and Serena Williams - both were ranked world No 1 in singles and doubles - was declared insane by many 'experts'. During practice, he constantly fed easy balls to his daughters, that bounced softly, half way up the court. The two sisters, with little physical exertion, could delightfully whack the balls into the corners with all their power, again and again. As they were allowed to play the balls from inside the baseline and not asked to constantly go back to the baseline to recover position, they had plenty of energy and time over to feel what it was like to hit those balls at full power, experience the joy of it and at the same time be aware of their technique. Now, seeing the exponential success both sisters have had, it can only be concluded that the father, by offering some exercises to them in this fashion, managed to generate 'the right feeling' whilst also working on technical transitions. Namely building confidence by doing what feels right without necessarily making the game situation realistic every time and without physically exhausting them. Giving them both enough time to really feel and see how the technique they were adjusting and becoming acquainted with, could be made to work and get the results they were after. This builds up confidence. Of course, it is also good to challenge a player by 'pushing' him/her physically, but forgetting to train 'the right feeling' regularly will come at the expense of self-confidence. It is important for players to feel powerful and learn to trust their technique in a fun, energetic way and at the same time be able to keep their concentration level exceptionally high. We highly recommend that you watch the film 'King Richard' where Wil Smith plays Richard Williams. It is a fascinating story of the exceptional Williams family.

You have to feel the technique first

Just as the Williams sisters trained their shots at a shorter distance than a full-length tennis court, and got fed balls that made it easier for them to execute their shots without exhausting them physically, it is also important to train new football skills in this way. When you do this, you will create a perfect situation in which you can consciously make changes from the right feeling. This is an underestimated approach in how to make improve your football skills and make technical progress in your game.

How do you do that on the football pitch?

From 2009 to 2018, Jackie trained young semi-professional football players in collaboration with Hesterine de Reus, Maria van Kortenhof and Roos Kwakkenbos, in preparation for their football careers. Jackie's role was to help the players become aware of the choice between Story Thinking and Action Thinking and finding and maintaining a mental balance during matches. Besides this mental awareness, it was extremely important to learn to train technically and tactically at the highest level.

Most players were used to doing a short warm-up, running around the pitch and catching up socially on what was going on outside of the pitch! Then moving slowly into the practice by kicking the ball back and forth gently without paying attention to detail or begin fully present. When you start this way, you attention is far from optimal and you are mostly in your head, meaning in thought and not in feeling. To change this, an awareness process must take place. The very first condition to enable technical progress from feeling is to be present right from the very moment you walk onto the pitch. In Intermezzo 1: 'A mental warming-up' you learn how to do this.

Once you are present in the warming-up you can immediately start becoming one with the ball, by feeling, listening and seeing how it touches your foot, the way it rolls over the ground, or spins in the air. You constantly bring yourself gently back to the now. From this point you will be able to make technical progress from feeling.

Be aware, what often happens in training when you start a technical exercise is that you have high expectations and might quickly get frustrated. This may be because you find repeating the exercise boring, or you are afraid you will never learn it, or that you don't pick up the skill quickly enough. Or that you have a constant doubt in the back of your mind, that no matter how much you practice, it will not go well in the match and you will not be selected to play. Or that another player in the team already has that skill and that makes you somewhat jealous. Often without realising it you are completely lost within your thoughts. All sorts of things are passing through your head that keep you stuck in Story Thinking instead of moving to Action Thinking and getting into the right feeling. Your attention is not exclusively with your technique.

When you are working on technique, it is necessary to be totally clear in what you want the technical change to look like. For example, on a specific pass, exactly which part of your foot needs to touch the ball first? And once you've seen that and decided clearly in your mind (visualisation) you then start to feel it, *literally physically feel it*, meaning that you do not look at the execution critically (thoughts, judgments). You are going to feel which part of your foot touches the ball and you are also going to see what the exact result is of what you are executing. The only way to do that excellently is to slow the game down, make things simple and small, not exhausting at the beginning, just in the same way that Richard Williams did with his world class daughters. Take the time to enjoy learning a new skill and encourage yourself to train from feeling instead of thought. You will be amazed at how this positively effects change.

Are you watching or thinking?

This sounds very logical, but Jackie noticed in many training sessions - both with individual athletes and team athletes at the highest level - that players forget to check what happens to the result of their effort after performing a technical change. How can that be? They are so caught up in their heads whether or not they are doing it right, whether or not they have understood the technical instructions correctly, that they neglect to see what has taken place. If you don't see what the result is, then you can never begin to feel what you need to do next with the technique to change and improve it.

Self-knowledge

Learning a new football skill takes time and needs patience. When players expect that changes in technique can be applied immediately in a match, that could be unrealistic. Having these expectations can put a dent in your self-confidence, instead of experiencing progress. Be kind to yourself, accept that if you give your all, that's where you are. Give your skills space to develop from feeling and not from thought!

Summary 'technical progress from feeling':

1. Check if you are present.
2. Prepare yourself mentally for the technical change you want to work on.
3. Then train from feeling: visualise exactly what you want to pay attention to? What part of your foot, hip or shoulder do you see executing the new skill and how? Feel your muscle tension, be aware of your breathing and know exactly where your eyes are. Do you feel where the ball touches your foot/head/chest? Are you being kind to yourself?
4. Track the result of exactly what you did with the ball. Scan and zoom.
5. If you don't manage to apply the change immediately in a match, that's ok, be kind to yourself and keep going, you are doing well.

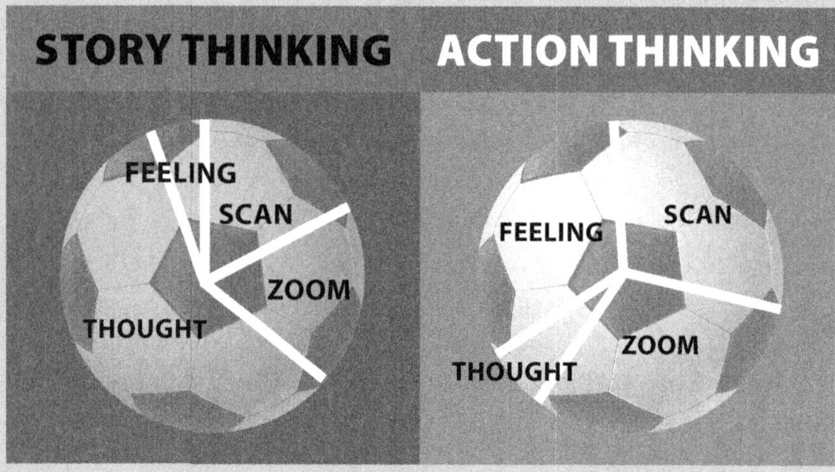

A man should look for what is, and not for what he thinks should be.

ALBERT EINSTEIN

CHAPTER 7

TACTICS ARE BASED ON FEELING

HOW DO I STAY ON TASK AND REMAIN TRUE TO TACTICS WITHOUT OVER THINKING?

This Chapter provides insight into the negative role of 'thinking too much' about your task and tactics. It offers a radically new perspective on how a player can keep to their task and be precisely focused on the agreed tactics.

Here is a question we have asked a great many athletes: Can you remember any time at which you were making tactically good choices but were not in control of your emotions? The answer is always 'No'!

So what can a player do to improve her tactical choices? *Learn to attach more value to the Instruments than to your thoughts.* Your emotions will then automatically become calmer and you will make better choices, from a clear presence of mind. If we look at the graph of the *Mindset* bird again, we can get a deeper understanding of why emotions affect tactics. Imagine if one of the wings suddenly fails: the bird will take a nose dive.

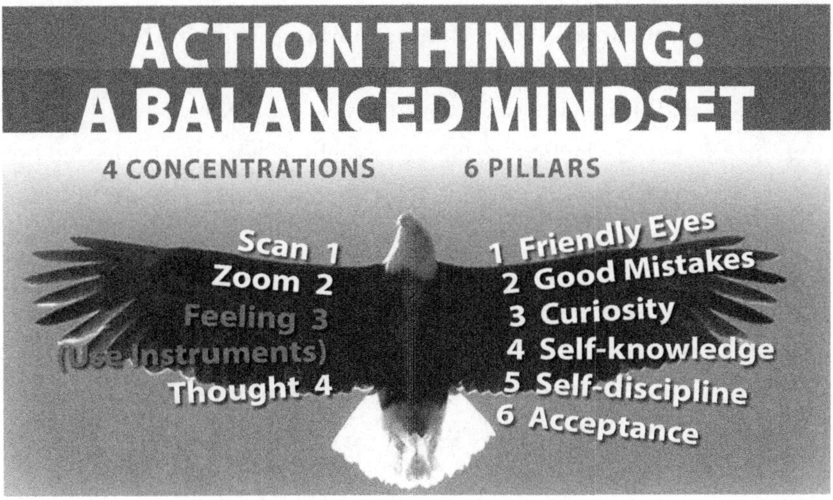

That is often the feeling a player gets when searching to play the right tactics. If either the concentration or the pillars are neglected, the players game falters. The bird can only fly smoothly when using both wings.

At all levels, you can see 'not being able to fly' happening. An inexperienced team, which clearly has players of inferior quality, but a team that has a passionate coach and players who get on well together and appreciate each other, is going up against a much more experienced team that has so far won everything. The supposedly stronger team thinks: 'We are going to crush this inexperienced team. They're lucky to be playing us and there's no way that they can score against us.'

Tactics from feeling in a match

The coach of the less experienced players opts for a strongly defensive tactic, namely the 1-5-3-2 formation. As the level of play is considerably different, she thinks this is the most efficient formation. Her team is inexperienced, but has a realistic self-image and is 100 per cent willing to play according to this tactic. The players encourage each other and focus on both team tactics and their own task, without being concerned with the result. The more experienced team does not manage to break through their defence and considers the game a farce. They go into total Story Thinking and are furious because thirty minutes have already passed and it is still 0 - 0. What they are thinking is written all over their faces; 'Surely we're not going to let these jokers get to half time without us scoring a goal! This is totally unacceptable.'

Half-time - Action Thinking or Story Thinking?

Half-time has been reached and it is still 0-0. Both teams go into half-time with two very different mindsets. One from 'tactics are based on thoughts' and the other from 'tactics are based on feeling'. The inexperienced but task-oriented members of the team with a realistic self-image come to the side and listen to their 'action-oriented' coach. She says: 'Ladies, you are doing well. Everybody is sticking to her task and the effort is 100 per cent. Keep it up and take your time to recover well so that we can give it our all again in the second half.' Then the coach is silent, because she knows the players need recovery time and room to conjure up how they see them themselves playing the second half. In practice matches, they have already trained lowering their breath and focusing on what is going well. The players are taking their time for themselves, eating and drinking a little, lowering their breathing and visualising how they will keep up the tactics in the second half too.

The experienced players are plagued. They walk off the pitch as if something terrible has happened. They can't believe they haven't scored yet and in their heads, they blame each other and also the coach. They have thoughts like 'this can't be true, we should be leading 4-0 against these numbskulls.' They let their shoulders hang and as they have a drink, the Story Thinking coach shouts at them: 'What are you doing, how many chances do you need to score? This makes no sense at all. Work harder and make sure you make the chances. We should never lose this match. I expect a lot more from you!'

The players are furious; they believe in what their coach says and feel totally fired up as they walk onto the pitch for the second half. They shout at each other: 'We are going to win this, let's make mincemeat out of them.'

The second half

The experienced players start playing more and more aggressively because of the coach's instructions combined with their frustration, and one of the players gets a red card. Some real doubt is now creeping in, even though the opponents 'are clearly nowhere near our level and are total numbskulls': 10 against 11 is difficult.

The Action Thinking coach calls to her captain: 'We are going to play 1-4-3-2, let the rest know and good luck. You can do it, believe in yourselves and keep giving everything.'

And so the game tilts. The experienced team has disappeared into almost only Story Thinking thoughts, the less experienced players carry on doing what was agreed upon and enjoy every action, even every moment. At five minutes before time, it's still 0-0 and out of total frustration the experienced team commits a foul in the penalty area. You can see the situation in front of you. The penalty is taken, the inexperienced team takes a 1-0 lead and time is almost up.

The match ends in 1 for the numbskulls - 0 for the experienced team! The supposedly better team had lost its tactical instinct and thus got lost its way on the pitch because Story Thinking was dominating every action;

they started judging instead of observing. They could have gotten themselves out of this predicament if they had implemented the Instruments to move them away from Story Thinking and into the feeling of Action Thinking. This almost certainly would have triggered a turnaround in the match. If players do not utilise the Instruments, and are unaware of the concentrations and pillars, their minds wonder to judgmental and fearful thoughts and there is no time or energy remaining to play the best tactic or to have laser sharp orientation skills with the use of scanning and zooming.

Thoughts during matches

Are the following thoughts, generated by uncertainty and fear, familiar to you while playing a match?

- My legs are feeling heavy
- What on earth am I doing here?
- Why am I doing this?
- Why is my strongest pass/shot letting me down now, of all times?
- I know I'm going to mess up again.
- We can't possibly win this.
- If we lose this match, we're going to give up playing altogether.
- If I play like this during matches, I will stop playing football.
- If Peter/Lucy continue playing at this level, it's a total waste of time me being on this team.
- Without a good coach, it's all pointless.

Almost all football players have thoughts like this. Negative emotions are deadly for finding the right tactics. That is because they focus on the perception of your own 'pain': for instance, your sense of unease because the tactic in a match is not going the way you had imagined. During football matches, thoughts should be used only for the purpose of remembering your task and chosen tactics. After that they must be disengaged to allow creativity and spontaneity to develop. The Instruments of Action Thinking help to release you from thoughts and rollercoaster emotions and to lead you to the right feeling, the here and now of a match. They help to shift your attention from concern about your own unease, pain and frustrations about yourself, your teammates and your opponents to the visual alertness and creativity and courage needed to freely play the chosen tactics. It is difficult to differentiate clearly, in tactics, between zoom, scan, feeling and thought, but the following table will nonetheless be useful in clarifying the different mindsets: Story Thinking versus Action Thinking. It was written from the perspective of a club player, but the same points essentially apply to professional players. NB. We assume here that professional players recognise the points made and can translate them to their own level of play on the basis of their own experience. The focus here is on how to gain tactical insight through positive emotions. These emotions ensure that your attention shifts to scanning and zooming: the ball, your teammates, the opponent, your own position and the opening in the field.

	Zoom	Scan	Feeling	Thought
Action Thinking	I see the keeper coming out of her goal and chip the ball over her.	I see that I am getting covered closely in the back from the left side and pass the ball back or turn to the right so that I can move forward with the ball.	I can feel the defender pushing me aside in a shoulder block. I do not flinch and choose to free myself up earlier and make more use of my speed. My trigger words are 'find space and accelerate.'	At half-time we received an instruction from the coach to switch play quicker as soon as we gain possession. I think briefly about what that means for my position and visualise exactly how I am going to do that: which lines I'll run, how I'm going to take possession and how I will pass in the depth.
Story Thinking	I see the keeper coming out of her goal and think 'Oh no, what should I do?' I then kick the ball straight into her body.	I see that I am getting covered closely in the back from the left side I think: 'How frustrating that I can't turn to my favourite side.'	I can feel the defender trying to pushing me aside with a shoulder block. Fear overwhelms me and I no longer see the spaces, I slow down and don't ask for the ball.	At half-time we received an instruction from the coach to to switch play quicker as soon as we gain possession. I know that I need to run faster and deeper but am afraid to be offside and ruin the attack for the team.

Tactical experiment with Mindset training on the football pitch

During Jackie's time working with young professional players, she experimented with the impact of trigger words (concentration form 'feeling') during matches. What impact did the trigger words have on tactics and on the individual level of play?

The experiment went as follows. Both teams were given tactical instructions from the coach and each player was aware of her personal task. The only difference was that one of the two teams was asked to internally regularly repeat the words 'Friendly Eyes' and 'Good Mistakes'. Also, when the moment was appropriate, to shout the words to their teammates. Without exception the team instructed to use the trigger words was more aware of what was happening in terms of tactics and had more energy left at the end of the match. The players also started to observe earlier than usual what the opponent was up to, which helped them see through the opponent's game patterns quicker. They also made quicker, better, more creative decisions about what they wanted to do with the ball. What caused this? The solutions came from the silence of Action Thinking rather than the noise of Story Thinking. By using Instruments to get into Action Thinking, they began to observe much better and they clearly performed at a higher level, with more fulfilment, than when their assignment was only concerned with tactics and task.

Turning thoughts into feeling and visual concentration is one of the most difficult skills in all disciplines. Up to the very highest level, footballers struggle with this. Yet everyone can (and should) use this information at her own level. This has everything to do with your willingness to work on the mental aspect step by step, be flexible and changing your mindset from Story Thinking to Action Thinking. Once you have mastered this, it becomes a fantastic cat-and-mouse game. Anyone can achieve this, but the *absolute prerequisites* are creativity and courage.

What is creativity and courage?

Being creative and courageous means constantly being on the lookout for possibilities, even when something painful happens (being behind in the match or physical exhaustion). Instead of holding on stubbornly or 'withdrawing', you look for a new way to keep yourself in Action Thinking and handle tactics intelligently. Often, a creative adaptation of your task in terms of tactics is the obvious choice, but it is crucial that you know how to muster the mental and physical energy required to make changes.

Sometimes you may try something out, but if it doesn't immediately work and you feel unsettled. You need to preserve your flexibility and learn to react on the basis of your observations.

The following two anecdotes illustrate the two opposite ways in which distracting thoughts may affect the player's creativity and courage.

Story Thinking club player

'During half-time I take a moment to reflect and am still convinced that I am a top striker as I am currently top scorer in the league. Normally I go pass the defence pretty easily with my swift actions. I don't understand it. In this match, that big, but slow defender always has an answer to my moves. I just don't seem to be able to get around them. How is that possible against such a slow player? I fear that if it continues like this, I will be taken off in the second half. The thought alone makes me despondent and angry.'

Action Thinking club player

'During half-time I take a moment to reflect. At this league level, they usually have no answer to my quick actions and I normally can create many opportunities. But this defender is hard to go around and almost always tackles me at the right moment. I will see if I can get around her/him by alternating more. I visualise on which side I will go around her/him in the second half. I see that I can surprise her/him in this way and that I will get the opportunity to score more often. Great.'

Story Thinking professional player

'During half-time I take a moment to reflect. I know I'm in shape and that I've faced this defender before. Normally I can get around them pretty often with my quick actions. The coach and I talked it through beforehand as we knew that he/she would be covering me and we decided how I would approach them. She/he is right-footed so eight times out of ten I would go around her on her left side. Why is it not working now? I just can't seem to get around him/her. If it continues like this then there's a good chance I'm going to be substituted. That's just terrible.'

Action Thinking professional player

'During half-time I take a moment to reflect and realise that when I try to go around my defender, I'm losing possession of the ball way too often. The tactic of trying to pass go around the left side is not working eight out of ten times, as it was in the previous game against her/him. I accept that and take a different approach. I choose to pass the ball earlier and more often to my teammates, so my defender doesn't always get the chance to react to my challenges. This forces her/him to divide their attention. Then, further into the match, I will make my actions towards the defender again. This will surprise her/him and I see myself going around her/him. This approach makes me feel strong and confident again.'

Creativity and courage involve constantly looking for new ways with the right mindset. As the anecdotes show, this is not always evident or easy, but it is always better than not changing anything at all or becoming despondent.

Why is it so difficult to stick to your task and to the chosen tactics?

It is difficult to stick to your task because you assume you can win with the game plan that is thought up beforehand. You assume that you can play the match either with conscious competence (cc) or even with unconscious competence (uc). During the game, you come to what can be a disappointing discovery: that you don't have all the qualities to execute the tactics successfully. Your own skills don't work (adequately) and you end up in conscious incompetent (ci) play. This often hurts. In daily life, you usually have enough time to think about problem situations and find a solution. While playing football, you don't have that time, or at most in very short periods.

Another reason why players find it so difficult to stick to their task and accomplish the agreed upon tactics is that they do not pay enough attention to what is going on with the opposing team and direct opponents. How the other team is playing can of course challenge the best tactical play and result in a lot of ball loss. Instead of allowing this to irritate or discourage you, it would be better to take a real interest in how their actions are succeeding. That is not always an easy thing to do.

Take an example that has nothing to do with football. Admittedly, this comparison may come across as rather far-fetched, but it may help you to define for yourself exactly what it is that is preventing you from acquiring tactical insight and being flexible.

A good friend confronts you with the fact that she finds you unreliable. This hurts you. You might react in a variety of ways:

1. You feel hurt, do not react at all in the first instance, and withdraw into your shell;
2. You get angry and say that no one else has this opinion of you;
3. You ask your friend where this accusation comes from.

As we know, many people react in the first or second way. This is comparable to what may happen during a match. You take too little interest in the cause, but react instead to what it does to you. Reactions 1 and 2 can be classified as Story Thinking, while reaction 3 is Action Thinking. Being curious about your opponent's game (compared here to your friend's feeling) in a non-judgmental way and without allowing yourself to feel crushed by the disappointing result, for example if your team is two goals down (compared here to the feedback provided by your friend) is a prerequisite for acquiring tactical insight. The pillar of curiosity is paramount.

'Tactics are based on feeling' in a nutshell

In football, everything you set out to do, the tactics, the actions, your task, seems to have only one goal: to win! But winning is in the future and the game is in the now. You will only be able to play at your highest level when you realise that by being in the now you will achieve the best results. By looking at tactics also as a feeling, you can be sure to stay in the now through Action Thinking. Visualising and trigger words are the best Instruments for transferring a 'devised' tactic into action. They help you quiet the thoughts of Story Thinking and bring you into the flow of Action Thinking.

ASSIGNMENTS FOR TACTICS

1. Visualise the following two situations for two minutes each:
   a. Everything is going well and you realise you are in a flow. Suddenly, because you start thinking, everything starts to slip away from you. How does that feel? What are the emotions that accompany it?
   b. Nothing is working and you're feeling desperate. What emotions accompany this situation? Can you conjure them up?

2. Conjure up the above two situations (1a and 1b) again, and see yourself becoming calm using your favourite Instruments and playing a strong tactical game.

Note! Remember that even during a match you can teach yourself to visualise like this.

3. What do you do to stay curious when the way you execute your task doesn't work? For example, you lose 7 out of 10 duels. How do you plan to stay 'curious' if this happens to you in a match?

4. In what respect do you consider that you possess creativity and courage during a match? Give two examples.

If you practise assignments number 1 and 2 regularly, your emotions will have far less strong a hold on you when these situations crop up in a match.They will have become more familiar and it will be easier for you to distance yourself from them. It's a fantastic discovery to realise that you can do this whenever and wherever you want. And it has so much added value. Raising your awareness in this way is the path of the Action Thinker.

FOOTBALL PASSION AND BICYCLE TYRES

DEFLATE OR INFLATE?

If a bicycle tyre is too slack you will have to pump it up, otherwise you will have difficulty moving forward. However, if you pump it up too hard, you have a bumpy ride and there is a risk of the tyre bursting. Then you have to allow a little air to escape. The key is to keep the tyre under the right pressure. The pressure must not be too high or too low. This is exactly how it works with your emotional balance.

There are three ways you can use your emotions to get/stay in Action Thinking:

1. Pumping yourself up;
2. Releasing tension: letting it out;
3. Doing nothing: you are calm and focused.

It is important that you learn to manage your emotions and know how to use them at the right moments to find balance and play with the right passion. Sometimes you will need to pump yourself up: this can be done by using words of encouragement or positive gestures that fire you up, like raising a clenched fist.

On other occasions you may want to 'let out' the pressure (which will therefore reduce the pressure) by releasing your feelings with a strong verbal response, a real shout of emotion or an expressive gesture. This can happen after a hard-fought duel, or any moment in the match when the pressure is building up strongly. An emotional cry or an exuberant jump into the air will release tension. Then there are other moments when it is good to stay calm and keep your emotions steady.

Many football players struggle to find this balance and often they learn it by trial and error. The important thing is to manage your emotions so as to cultivate the right amount of passion, which induces Action Thinking. This too is trainable.

Every player needs to be aware of this balance and capable of understanding how to 'inflate and deflate' their energy levels when needed. You will notice that many world class players know instinctively how to use these three methods of emotional management to play consistently with passion throughout the whole match.

Pumping yourself up too much or too little, releasing tension too much or too little, keeping too much or too little composure: they cause the player to move from Action Thinking to Story Thinking. Passion is an indispensable condition in football, but passion also needs to be used in the right proportion.

During *Mindset* trainings, we practice passion by learning to express emotions in different ways and moments - regardless of the result. The effect of this is immediate and positive: the players often feel liberated and gain insights to how their energy works by playing with their emotions in this way.

Expressions of passion at different moments in a match:

1. *Pump the tyre up*: Pumping yourself up: you feel yourself becoming a little passive, you encourage yourself when you feel your energy level lacking. After executing a great pass, you express yourself with something that invigorates you: for instance, you say 'Come on!' or 'Allez!' to yourself, raising a clenched fist. This causes a release of adrenaline, a hormone that is essential to induce the best possible focus and to play with and the necessary energy.
2. *Release some pressure*: Release, let it out – jump in the air, shake all of your muscles loose and release a huge scream of victory after a crucial moment in the match. For example, an amazing action that leads to a corner. You feel the tension drain from your body. This moment of release helps you to calm down and will not go unnoticed by the opposing team.

3. *Getting the tension right*: You know you're playing a good match; you choose not to express yourself, since you feel that the emotional tension is just right.

We would like to motivate coaches and players alike to make 'passion' a regular part of their program by training it in practice sessions. The more a football player becomes aware of the power of 'passion' the more likely that she will be able to reproduce this in a match situation.

We suggest three identical exercises of three minutes each. Every three minutes change the way you express your emotions after an action:

1. You pump yourself up;
2. You really let it out (so that the opponent can hear);
3. You stay calm.

A happy man is too satisfied with the present to dwell too much on the future.

ALBERT EINSTEIN

CHAPTER 8

ODYSSEUS AND THE LOTUS-EATERS

HOW CAN I GET INTO A FLOW?

Becoming conscious, one step at a time, of what it means to be in a 'flow', or the 'zone', and of how you can create the conditions needed to achieve it.

When the Trojan War finally comes to an end, Odysseus sets sail for his beloved Ithaca and his wife Penelope. It is to be a long and arduous journey, full of strange exploits and perils. When he and his crew come to the isle of the lotus-eaters (which scholars have identified as Jerba, an island off the coast of Tunisia) he sends scouts to check out the local population. The Greek scouts eat the unfamiliar lotus flowers offered to them, which cause them to forget their homeland and to want to stay on the island. Their sole desire is to carry on eating the flowers and to bask in blissful oblivion. Odysseus has to use force to get them to leave and to continue their voyage.

Paradise or true happiness?

The lotus-eaters' paradise may sound like an attractive place to be, but does it really hold out the ultimate fulfilment that people desire? Is this fulfilment not simply a banal drug addiction that ultimately makes you into a zombie and keeps you in a crippling state of numbness and darkness? To achieve real fulfilment and happiness, Odysseus and his companions have to perform their task and cannot allow themselves to succumb to the intoxication of pleasure. The psychologist Mihaly Csikszentmihalyi (pronounce 'chick-sent-me-high-ee'!) has demonstrated scientifically that human beings feel happiest not in a drugged-up state of lethargic well-being, but in a state of heightened alertness and clarity, which he calls 'flow'. Csikszentmihalyi describes flow as a state of complete absorption in an activity. At the same time, your skills are being tested to the utmost. The challenge of the task must be appropriate to the skill of the person performing it (challenge-skill balance, in Csikszentmihalyi's terms). If the task is too easy or too difficult, no flow can develop, he explains.

The purpose of Zen and other forms of meditation is to achieve this ideal alertness and clarity. And that is also exactly what we try to attain in football. It is also called 'presence of mind': the elimination of past and future, and the total immersion in the here and now. In short, it means achieving total presence and complete awareness. The ego disappears, and a state of 'no mind' comes into being. People who never meditate will also recognise this feeling, from sport, music, work or cooking. You forget time completely, are utterly absorbed in what you are doing, and experience a 'buzz' of happiness. In sport, this feeling is usually called flow, or 'being in the zone'. Both terms refer to the same state, one in which everything seems to be going automatically and you are working at the peak of your ability. Flow can't be willed or commanded into existence; you can't decide 'to spend some time in the zone'. What you can do, however, is to put in place the right conditions – the conditions that can enable you to end up 'in the zone', to experience flow during a match. This Chapter is devoted to the subject of flow and the way in which these ideal conditions can be created.

Shameless consumerism

If not linked to a goal, the glorification of living in the here and now may lead to shameless consumerism. If Odysseus's scouts had carried on endlessly devouring lotus flowers, it would not have made them happy in the end. Eventually they would have experienced a sense of frustration, as happens to drug addicts and alcoholics. On the football pitch too, there is a consumerism that produces frustration. This point has already been raised (in Chapter 1) in relation to the mindset of the 'malfunctioning machine' and in Chapter 2 on the issue of consumerism versus investment.

Some players think they are entitled to play well if they put in enough hours. Others see football skills as a product that can be purchased. They go to the 'right' club with an experienced coach and great training programme, and then expect to be automatically provided with the next level skill set. Then, if they find that the product turns out to be defective, when playing a match, they take their 'malfunctioning machine' back to the 'shop' (i.e., the coach) to be mended. They fail to appreciate that to make progress in their own game, they will also need to work on themselves. More importantly, they do not understand how exciting and rewarding this self-development can be.

Your fate is largely held in your own hands. The fact that so much depends on yourself is not frustrating but rather challenging and satisfying. Of course, what's great about football is that you might be fortunate to have the entire team at your side to help you stay on the right track. This makes things extra special. (see Intermezzo 2).

How can I get into a flow?

How you achieve the wonderful state of flow? It is a state in which everything goes automatically, as if body and mind have come together and you can trust wholly to the skills 'in your suitcase'. Story Thinking is completely absent, and Action Thinking takes over completely. Chapters 5 and 6 discussed in detail the way in which you can achieve Action Thinking and the obstacles that need to be overcome. Feeling is the bridge you need to go from thought to the visual. For instance, you can use your own trigger words as bridges to go from thought to the correct kind of alertness (external: scanning and zooming). *Flow is only possible by using external concentration.*

Bear in mind that you will not experience flow if you start thinking about it. You can't force it.

What are the conditions for getting into a flow?

Challenge

One important condition for achieving flow is that you have a big enough challenge; otherwise, boredom may set in. That is why it is so important to set yourself goals. Make sure that you always have a clear picture in your mind of your goals in a match or training session, goals that ensure that you are really challenged. Formulate a realistic challenge for yourself and focus all your attention on it. Check with your coach and teammates if your goal is correct. Luckily, in football this is always possible. Even so, players often slip into a state in which it is extremely unlikely that they will ever get into the zone. There is nothing wrong with 'just kicking the ball around', but don't expect this ever to give you the euphoria that comes with the state of flow.

If you find yourself playing against a far weaker opponent, think up something that will help you to stay focused. For instance, pass, when possible, every ball with a technique that you would not normally dare to use. This will constantly challenge you to get into the right position before passing the ball. If your opponent is much stronger, set yourself realistic goals. For example, aim to enter every duel with the trigger words 'I give everything and dare'. This will keep you sharp throughout the match, no matter how many times you 'win' or 'lose' the duel. See this commitment as a victory. It ensures you keep your energy up and maybe you will unconsciously end up in a flow. That cannot be your goal, because again: the right mindset does not consist of *thinking* and desiring. You can get into a flow if you give quality to all your actions and are in the now.

Realistic self-image

The positive balance needed between challenge and skills can arise only if you have a *realistic self-image*. Take the following example. A player whose team draws in a match against a 'lesser' team, walks off the pitch furious and says: 'That's really not football, I can't believe we drew against those losers! So many chances, huge bummer. Luckily we're playing a better team next week, because I can't cope with that fumbling around at this level!' This clearly falls under the category of 'mentally unconscious incompetent'. What is striking about this example is that it happens more often than you think. Even among semi-professional players, such thoughts occur. It might be that many players don't dare to say these things out loud, though inwardly they do react in this way. We know this from years of experience with young semi-professional players. Be aware, it is very unlikely that a player who thinks in this fashion will experience a flow in matches. An unrealistic self-image can only lead to even more frustration and worse play. Chapter 9 will help you set realistic goals and teach you how to strive to get into a flow.

The here and now

It is also important to remember that *action and consciousness* will only *come together* if you can switch off the 'thinking ego' of Story Thinking and operate wholly in the *here and now*. If you can do so, you will find yourself not thinking about your movements, but performing them effortlessly and 'automatically'. Earlier Chapters have already discussed ways of escaping from Story Thinking and switching to Action Thinking. Once you have achieved this, you have created conditions in which the state of flow can be experienced.

Winning or having the best possible experience?

If your goal is to win a match and this win fails to materialise, the result is a sense of frustration. But if your goal is to perform as well as possible, you can still feel satisfied after losing a match, and even experience flow. The reason for this, of course, is that this mindset will help you get into the *here and now*; feeling that you 'must win' focuses your mind on the future, and therefore takes you away from Action Thinking. Flow can only be experienced in the here and now. Fear of losing will often hold you back: you will be risk-averse, and won't deploy your skills to the best of your ability. On the other end of the scale, complacency may mean that you stop challenging yourself, which blunts the alertness you need to perform well.

Letting your ego go

The main obstacle on the path to experiencing flow is your ego. The 'loss of ego' that occurs during flow is liberating, and may be compared to different forms of meditation. This experience can also teach us that it is evidently possible to live without the ego (to many people a terrible thought) and that this could actually produce a state of perfect well-being. It teaches us that by letting the ego go and engaging deeply with life, we can feel happy as well as achieving more. 'Letting go' is the key here; trying to impose solutions will impede the ability to experience flow.

People who meditate, and who are familiar with this attempt to 'lose the ego', will have less difficulty letting go of their egos during a match, since the ego will not allow itself to be suppressed so easily. In fact, the ego's most striking characteristic is precisely that it is always trying to expand, and will strongly repel any efforts to suppress it. The ego feeds on judgments and hostilities. These vanish in a state of flow. During a flow experience, actions are steered by the faculty of observation, not judgment. Any intervention by the ego will disturb that perfect chiming of action and consciousness. There is no place for the ego in Action Thinking.

What exactly is 'the ego'?

We have used the word 'ego' several times now, each time in rather negative terms. But what exactly do we mean by the word 'ego'? The ideas on the ego presented in this book have been distilled from our experiences with meditation. The ego is a complex concept that is surrounded by many mysteries. Still, we do not believe it can be left out of consideration, since it plays an important role in our philosophy. How should the concept of the 'ego' be understood? How do we see it in relation to our ideas regarding the mental challenges of football?

The ego is a mental construct from which we believe that we can derive our identity. It derives completely from a person's past and future. In the course of our lives, we form views, opinions, and judgments about others and about ourselves, and from this chaotic jumble we compose a picture, which we call our identity. The ego exists *by virtue of its difference* from other egos; difference is what gives the ego its raison d'être.

The ego lives on Story Thinking. In fact, you could say that ego and Story Thinking are inseparable partners. Since the ego's biggest enemy is the here and now, and since the ego is wholly dependent on the past and the future, ego and flow are incompatible.

Relating this to sport, you might say that the ego shows its face most clearly in the thoughts of Story Thinking (judgmental, hostile, irrational or excessive thoughts with which the ego identifies).

As soon as you allow the following points to sink in, the ego will lose its force and be replaced by unconscious and automatic responses.

Action Thinking = loss of ego

1. Thoughts arising from pure observation, without being attached to any judgment. These thoughts are short, purposeful and clear.
2. Feeling by applying the Instruments (eye control, rituals, breathing, etc.).
3. The visual (zooming and scanning).

Yoga

Many people find it hard to tell the difference between tense and relaxed muscles. Alex Morgan says: 'I love doing Yoga to put my mind away from soccer. I do it because it will help me during playing soccer.' Yoga can teach you this. Yoga consists of techniques of switching back and forth between tension and relaxation – physical as well as mental – by means of breathing and physical exercises. It teaches you to focus your energy constructively and to calm your story thinking mind. Yoga also helps you to quickly become aware of the emotions that may take control of you – during and outside football. Physical and breathing exercises can help you to quickly identify these emotions and determine what you want to do with them. Since you learn to recognise your physical limits better, you also learn to distinguish between different kinds of pain. Some teachers differentiate between 'green' and 'red' pain. Green pain is pain you should be aware of but that can be ignored (not denied). Red pain should sound an immediate alarm and generally warns you to stop playing immediately. Pain must never be denied since that causes stress and it is dangerous for your body. In both green and red pain, learn to relax and breathe through the pain. Yoga can teach you to feel the difference between the different pains, and you will learn what breathing through the pain means. There are many different kinds of yoga. *Hatha yoga* is the most common and popular kind in the Western world. It consists of physical exercises and techniques that foster breathing, balance, relaxation and concentration. The aim is to help you to feel more balanced and energised. An added advantage is that yoga improves the flexibility of your body.

Many professional players are now aware of the benefits of yoga and have become dedicated practitioners. When Ajax (the famous Dutch football team) won the Champions League, the players started their training sessions with the yoga sequence known as the 'Sun salutation'.

Their fitness coach Laszlo Jambor was well ahead of his times, introducing this technique into the rather traditional world of football as early as 1995. In 1996 and 1997, Laszlo worked together with Jackie coaching talented tennis children. He taught Jackie the value of the sun salutation and how important it is to focus on detail. In 2014, the coach of the Dutch women's hockey team, Max Caldas, invited Jackie and Jacqueline van Meyel, to prepare the team mentally for the World Championships using the *Mindset* method. The Championships took place on home ground in the Netherlands. The team had won gold at the last two Olympic Games, so the expectations were high and the coach and team wanted to do everything possible to be able to handle the pressure and stay in the here and now.

One of the things we developed together with the team was the pre-match ritual. We practiced the sun salutation together until it was as good as 'perfect'. The team stood in a circle and each player, at their own speed, performed every movement with great attention. The focus was on breathing, eye control and muscle tension, thus shutting off the world around them and being in control of 'their own energy'.

At the same time, by being in the circle, they felt connected to each other. We practised this before and after every training session. When the World Championship arrived, they were ready. This ritual made sure that they started the matches from the right 'feeling'.

The team won the World Championships. After the tournament, some of the experienced players stated that they had enjoyed the match challenge more than in the past. They also expressed that it was fun and practical to train their mindset.

Meditation

Although meditation may seem far removed from football, and even the opposite kind of activity, there are more similarities between them than you might think. Meditation is a perfect way of learning how not to identify with your thoughts or emotions. It teaches you that you have a *choice*: you do not have to be controlled by your thoughts or feelings, you can learn how to create mental space through which you can choose your mindset. However difficult this may be, and however much practice it requires, it is possible to struggle free from the jumble of thoughts and emotions that seem to control you. For example: I don't dare to take on the tackle. To speak in the terms of this book, it is possible to escape from Story Thinking and to shift to Action Thinking, *as soon as you realise that you can choose not to identify with your thoughts or feelings.* In our view, meditation is an ideal aid in achieving this. More and more prominent football players and world class athletes from all fields, use different kinds of meditation and yoga as part of their training. The difference they feel in their well-being and performance level, experienced as a result of meditating daily is now scientifically supported. Due to advances in neuropsychology and MRI scans, we can now literally see what changes the brain undergoes when training with commitment.

Why Erling Haaland meditates

Erling Haaland says in an interview with Esporte Interativo: 'I like to meditate, it's been helping me a lot to find an inner peace, so it's been good for me.'

Erling has brought meditation into his game, he even celebrates some of his goals by sitting down cross legged, in a meditation position. Many players have imitated Erling's celebrational ritual by mocking him and also taking on the same position after a goal. Erling does not react to this, he knows how important it is to observe without judgment and due to this has learned what is worth reacting to and what not!

Scientific research

It has been proven that meditation reduces tension and heightens consciousness. One of the studies was done by Sara Lazar, a neuroscientist from Harvard Medical School. A group of people, who had never meditated before, agreed to practice for forty minutes daily for a period of eight weeks. Brain scans show that parts of their brains thickened in this period giving the following benefits. Meditators made better executive decisions (think of tactics) and became more compassionate to others and themselves (Friendly Eyes). The only part of their brain that became smaller (an added bonus) was their amygdala (the 'fright and flight' part of the brain). Meaning they will have less fear under pressure.

What can happen during meditation?

Specific techniques in meditation will help you raise your awareness and be able to choose to let go of external and internal influences that arise. You learn to perceive thoughts without judgment and allow them to float by. Meditation is an excellent way to learn to recognise that you have a choice between Story Thinking and Action Thinking. By practicing daily, you not only learn to raise your awareness (applying the pillars properly) but also to focus on exactly where you want your attention to be (feeling instead of thoughts, the Instruments).

We often receive the following feedback concerning meditation practice: 'I managed to spend a few weeks working on my mindset and I was aware of the benefits of Action Thinking, but I kept falling back into my old patterns of Story Thinking.' We highly recommend using meditation as a daily guide to constantly remind you to that Action Thinking is the way forward. It is proven that meditation reduces tension and increases your awareness. Be aware that during the exercises you are investing and not consuming. Understanding the role of the six pillars will support and encourage your meditation practice and help you through trial and error whilst exploring the mind.

Consider the effect that the shadow side of the pillars can have. The following examples will give you a rough idea of what consuming rather than investing can do to your mindset when it comes to meditation.

- UnFriendly Eyes instead of Friendly Eyes: 'I can't sit still for more than 5 minutes; this really gets on my nerves and I get angry with myself';
- Unaware mistakes instead of Good Mistakes: 'I can't focus on my breath for more than 10 seconds; after that my thoughts start shooting off in all directions. But I'm fine with that, it will improve by itself, I'm totally zen.'
- Indifferent instead of curious: 'Meditation is only for softies and spiritual people; it wouldn't work for me.'
- Unrealistic self-image instead of self-knowledge: 'I could do it every day if I wanted to, but I have different priorities.'
- Routine instead of self-discipline: 'I meditate for 5 minutes when I have time, but I'm too busy at the moment.'

- Frustration and unreal self-image instead of acceptance: 'I gave meditation a chance, and it's not my thing. I could tell after practicing for 5 minutes.'

Buddhist texts often refer to transformations of consciousness. There are many parallels between this idea and what we refer to here as a change of mindset, from story to Action Thinking. Read what Joseph Goldstein says about meditation in his book *Insight Meditation*, and see how easily this can be translated into our assertions about that mental switch.

'First of all we take a close look at this heart-mind to see what is what. Through the careful practice of observing, we develop a discriminating wisdom, so that we understand for ourselves what mental states are unskilful, that is, leading to suffering, and what states are skilful, leading to happiness.'

What is suffering? What is happiness? These are big words, but let's try to define answers that clarify the link with this book. Suffering arises when you identify too strongly with your thoughts and emotions, from the ego, from being judgmental, from Story Thinking. Happiness can be found in acceptance, letting go, selflessness, the now, non-judgmental observation, Action Thinking.

Meditation can help to transform Story Thinking into Action Thinking. Suffering doesn't need to disappear, but acceptance gives suffering a completely different feeling... the feeling of Action Thinking!

Soft skill of hard work?

For some readers, this Chapter may be difficult to follow. They have thoughts such as: 'meditation is not my cup of tea' or 'it's good, I know, but I can't do it' or 'I wouldn't know how to meditate.'

We ask everyone to remain curious. Many people consider meditation as a 'soft skill'. The opposite is true. Sitting still daily is a challenge and hard work! Only when you have the courage to face your own thoughts, positive change can happen. Meditation will undoubtedly help you further in this regard.

In conclusion - if you want to be part of the *Mindset* Revolution, take action! Choose your *Mindset* goal in the next Chapter and start your 6 week success plan.

ASSIGNMENTS ON FLOW AND EGO

1. Have you ever experienced a flow? If so, describe it. If not, try and describe why you think you might not have and how you could change this?
2. Do you think that your ego plays a role during matches? If so, what role does it play, and what is your opinion about this?
3. Do you mind losing? If so, why? Whose opinion matters most? Do you care on your own account, or do you care about the reaction of your coach, your team, your friends, your parents, your partner or other external factors?
4. Before a game, have you ever thought: 'that team is too strong, we can never beat them' or 'that team is so weak, we can never lose to them'. If so, what could you do now to be better prepared for the match and create the opportunity to get into a flow?

ONLINE MEDITATION COURSE GUIDED BY JACKIE REARDON

You can only begin to understand meditation by doing it. Using the methodology of this book, a three-month online meditation course has been developed under Jackie's guidance. The course is called 'Experience'.

Not convinced yet? Read the online reviews, many professional performers and club players have gone before you. The course is based on donation, as this universal knowledge must be made available for all. Be part of the revolution; make improving your mindset through kindness a daily responsibility. A whole new world will open for you.

www.friendlyeyes.com

I must be willing to give up what I am in order to become what I will be.

ALBERT EINSTEIN

CHAPTER 9

CHOOSE YOUR MINDSET GOAL

A SUCCESS PLAN FOR ACTION THINKING

Only when you decide and specify what your mental goal is, will there be a real possibility for improved concentration and mental growth through kindness. Let's get started!

Take your time to answer the questions and read the instructions carefully before delving deep into your consciousness to choose your *Mindset* goal.

When you stick to your plan and commit to practising daily for 5 minutes in the morning and evening, for a period of six weeks, you are bound to make progress. You will be monitoring and reflecting on your chosen goal daily. Your concentration will improve and you will experience positive change. You will train both wings of the bird – the pillars, the concentrations and the Instruments – by doing this you will learn to acquire a balanced mind.

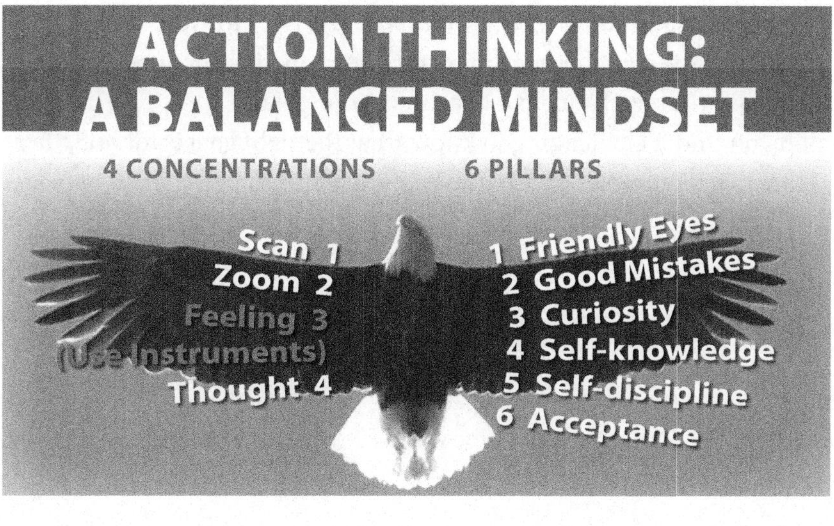

Below you see the concentration pie, to remind you to train your mindset from 'feeling instead of thought'. Trust yourself, let all expectations go for now and just follow the plan set out in this book. After six weeks you will have experienced what training from 'feeling instead of thought' is and it will be clear what it has brought you.

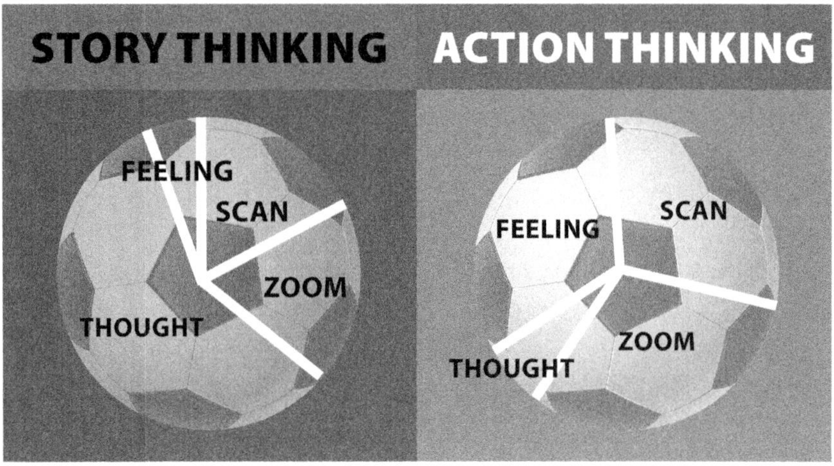

START NOW!

1. Answer all of the following questions to acquire knowledge that will help you in deciding which *Mindset* goal is right for you.
2. After answering the questions, then read the instructions of how to choose your goal and how to achieve your goal.
3. If you find it challenging to know what the right goal is for you, there are many examples of *Mindset* goals to help you figure it out on pages 211 to 218.

1. Describe a specific situation when you were in Action Thinking. Describe how it felt.

2. Describe a specific situation when you were in Story Thinking. Describe how it felt.

3. Looking back on your answer to the question about Story Thinking: what would you do differently now to bring yourself away from Story Thinking and into Action Thinking if the situation were to repeat itself. *(If you believe that it is not possible to change anything, discuss this with others. The Discover Course and the Mindset books are meant to give insight in how to change Story Thinking to Action Thinking.)*

4. The mindset-vision states: 'Winning from yourself is more important than winning from your opponent' and 'If you think in terms of winning or losing you're in a position of dependency. If you give quality to all your actions, the results will come by themselves.' How would this affect your situation if you took these statements to heart?

5. **Assignment 5a and 5b** are meant to help you develop self-knowledge and assist you in choosing a specific, realistic and positive mental goal. We are all constantly switching between Story and Action Thinking. By doing the following assignments you create clarity in your patterns. Both assignments consist of the following three steps:
Step 1: Ask a coach / manager / colleague / partner or friend to complete the left column of both the tables below on this page and the next.
Step 2: Now complete the right column of the tables yourself, without looking at the ratings in the left column.
Step 3: Once you have completed the two assignments, compare them on how you scored yourself in the different categories. If you scored low in Story Thinking for a specific category and high in Action Thinking for the opposing category (example: judging yourself = 2, Friendly Eyes for self=5) you can consider this to be a strength. If the score is the other way around – high in Story Thinking and low in Action Thinking – see this as something you might need to improve on.

To complete the two tables, use the following scale to grade yourself (or the person you are assessing) on when you (or the person you are assessing) are in a story- or action-thinking mood:
1=low (hardly ever) 3=moderate (sometimes) 5=high (almost always).

5a. This assignment helps you to develop self-knowledge:

Coach/colleague/friend/partner *You*

Story Thinking	1	2	3	4	5	Story Thinking	1	2	3	4	5
judging yourself						*judging yourself*					
judging others						*judging others*					
unaware mistakes						*unaware mistakes*					
indifference						*indifference*					
ignorance						*ignorance*					
boredom						*boredom*					
complacency						*complacency*					
negative						negative					
insecure						insecure					
giving up						giving up					
impatient						impatient					
full of doubt						full of doubt					
apathetic						apathetic					
stubborn						stubborn					
fearful						fearful					
predictable						predictable					
dependent						dependent					
easily distracted						easily distracted					

5b. Ask your coach/manager/colleague/partner or friend to fill in the left hand side of the chart for you, this time for when you are in an action-thinking mood:

1=low (hardly ever) 3=moderate(sometimes) 5=high (almost always).

Coach/colleague/friend/partner *You*

Action Thinking	1	2	3	4	5	Action Thinking	1	2	3	4	5	
Friendly Eyes for self						*Friendly Eyes for self*						6 Pillars
Friendly Eyes for others						*Friendly Eyes for others*						
Good Mistakes						*Good Mistakes*						
curiosity						*curiosity*						
self-knowledge						*self-knowledge*						
self-discipline						*self-discipline*						
acceptance						*acceptance*						
positive						positive						
self-confident						self-confident						
persevering						persevering						
patient						patient						
with conviction						with conviction						
motivated						motivated						
flexible						flexible						
courageous						courageous						
creative						creative						
autonomous						autonomous						
focused						focused						

CHOOSING YOUR GOAL

How do you identify the goal best suited to you, to increase your mental awareness and to enhance your performance? You can begin by looking back at the assignments you have carried out on the last two pages. Compare your scores to those of your coach and partner, these will give you a good general direction and help you define the right mental goal. You don't necessarily have to choose what is in the chart. More importantly is that you feel excited about the choice you make and that you realise what the benefits will be if you manage to bring improvement to this mental aspect. Also ask your coach what she/ he feels you should work on. If you find it difficult to decide, don't worry, just choose one of the traits from Story Thinking that you want to convert to Action Thinking.

How many goals should I choose?

Please choose one mental goal at a time for six weeks, you can reuse this book as many times as you like. If for example you choose to be more patient, braver and be more disciplined all at the same time, you are setting yourself up for failure, as these are not realistic goals to achieve in six weeks. Choose one goal to focus on, monitor it and you will improve. After six weeks, you can repeat the same goal or choose another one. When you do this over a period of 1 year, can you imagine what you can achieve!

To help you formulate your own mindset goal there are many examples written on pages 211 to 218. They show you how to create new habit patterns for better concentration and enjoyment under pressure.

HOW TO ACHIEVE YOUR MINDSET GOAL

The basis of your training is to combine the two pillars (Friendly Eyes and Good Mistakes) with four Instruments: rituals, breathing, visualisation and trigger words. You start the day by reading 'what you want to achieve'. Then you lower and deepen your breath for three minutes. Only after lowering your breath do you start to visualise your goal and how you are going to achieve it for two minutes. Finally, your trigger words will remind you of what you want to focus on during the day.

Friendly Eyes and Good Mistakes

In the Discover course and the books, we have talked extensively about learning to observe without judgment and that it is necessary for you to make mistakes. Without this foundation it is extremely difficult to make mental progress and even when you do, it won't feel great. That is why these two pillars are so important and offer the foundation to achieving your *Mindset* goal. Apply them, be honest about how you're doing, but also be kind to yourself and be understanding when you're not always doing what you set out to do. Don't judge yourself, but keep believing in achieving your goal using Friendly Eyes and Good Mistakes.

THE INSTRUMENTS

Rituals

Your ritual is to read what your goal is every morning and to reflect on how your attention went daily in the evening by filling in the daily success plan on the following pages. If you put this book next to your bed you will heighten your chances of remembering to execute this ritual.

Every morning, preferably at the same time, just after you get up, pay attention to your *Mindset* goal for one minute, read consciously 'what do I want to achieve' then continue with the exercises explained below.
Every evening before you go to bed, reflect on how your practice went. Did you focus on your goal, if so, what did you notice, if not why not?

Take 5 minutes to reflect and give yourself a grade for each part of the mental training.

Trigger word(s)

Your trigger word(s) is linked to your chosen goal. You use it during the day to consistently remind yourself what you want to focus on and what you are trying to achieve.

Breath

By slowing down, deepening and lowering your breath daily for 3 minutes in the morning, your parasympathetic nervous system will be influenced in a positive way. When you breathe between 6 and 9 times per minute (in and out counts as one time), you will make better decisions and see more clearly what you want to achieve. Therefore, it is extremely important to first lower and slow your breath before you start visualising. In this way, you approach your goal from Action Thinking.

Breathing exercise - every morning

Take an active, sitting position with your hands on your belly. Set the timer for **3 minutes**. Close your eyes, focus on your breathing. Breathe in and out through your nose. Make sure your breathing is as gentle and as deep as possible, without forcing it. Feel your hands rise and fall. Don't worry if you have restless thoughts or if you find the task difficult. Look at yourself with Friendly Eyes and start again, again and again. Be concerned only with lowering and deepening your breathing. Let all other thoughts pass you by and return to your breathing.

Visualise what I will do differently to achieve my goal

After you have done the breathing exercise, visualise for **2 minutes** each morning exactly what you want from yourself and what behavior you expect from yourself in relation to your *Mindset* goal. For example: I visualise that I act differently when I am criticised. I open up and am curious about what I've been told and see it as positive criticism. Instead of reacting in an irritated way and going onto the defence, I react with Friendly Eyes and ask an open question if I don't understand what the other person is trying to point out to me. By doing this I see that my relationship with others changes and I will learn more from their feedback.

HOW DOES IT WORK?

1. Mindset Goal - what do I want to achieve?
Choose one goal, make sure that it is specific, positive and realistic.

2. What is holding me back?
Define what is preventing you from achieving your goal, or has prevented you in the past. Also ask what people close to you think is holding you back. Be open and honest, see all feedback as a way to improve.

3. What do I stand to gain if I work on my chosen goal?
Write down what benefits you would derive from working on your chosen goal. By reflecting daily on your goal and the benefits it will bring, it makes it easier to persevere.

4. How am I going to achieve this?

a. Begin every morning by reading carefully 'what do I want to achieve'.
b. Use Friendly Eyes and Good Mistakes as the foundation of your change.
c. Choose a trigger-word that reminds you of your goal. Put the trigger word in a place where you constantly see it. For example, in the opening screen of your mobile phone and on a piece of paper in your sport bag.
d. Lower and deepen your breath every morning for 3 minutes.
e. Visualise exactly what you expect from yourself and will do differently to achieve your goal. Do this every morning for 2 minutes
f. In the evening, reflect on how your focus was during the day and give yourself a grade. (1=unaware, 5= highly aware).

5. Who do I choose as my buddy and which day do I get feedback?
Choose one person, a buddy, to encourage you and check your progress, always with Friendly Eyes! When your commitment also involves someone else, you are twice as likely to keep to it. Agree a set time in the week when you speak to your buddy to give and get feedback on how you are doing with your goal.

6. Chosen period of time
I practice daily for 6 weeks from ___/___/20__ until ___/___/20__

EXAMPLE OF A MINDSET GOAL

1. What do I want to achieve?

To be bolder and more daring at all moments in the match. The score will not affect my choices.

2. What is holding me back?

The fear of making mistakes or of making the wrong decision. The tenser it gets, the more cautiously I play. I just don't seem to have the courage to attempt a long pass, or make a strong tackle. I lose trust in myself and feel awful.

3. What do I stand to gain if I work on my chosen goal?

More self-respect and trust in myself to make the long passes and tackles, by taking clear decisions at key moments. I'll enjoy the game more and get better results. This will bring better contact with my coach and teammates.

4. How am I going to achieve this?

a. Begin every morning by reading carefully: 'what do I want to achieve'.

b. I approach my mindset goal with Friendly Eyes and Good Mistakes. When I am confronted with a pressure situation and 'tense up' again, I understand that this is all part of the process and is ok. It takes time to change. I immediately stop punishing myself and continue with my plan.

c. Trigger words: Be bold and daring. I put them on the opening screen of my mobile and stick them on the mirror in the in the bathroom.

d. Breathing: every morning I lower and deepen my breath for 3 minutes.

e. I visualise every morning for 2 minutes that I take risks in situations where I would normally hold back. I create an exact match situation in my mind's eye and see myself passing the ball freely and with precision. I see myself making an amazing tackle and gaining possession. After all actions, I walk with my head straight and my shoulders back. The result of my actions does not affect my posture. If I notice any tension, I take 3 deep breaths and tell myself 'you are bold and daring. I feel great about this new approach and confident that I will improve.

f. In the evening I reflect on how my goal went and how the day was and score myself using the chart. (1=unaware, 5= highly aware).

5. Who is my buddy and when do I get feedback?

I'll ask my teammate Rory if they'll be my buddy.

6. My six-week period is from: ___/___/20__ until ___/___/20__

NAME: Kelly Peters
WHAT DO I WANT?: To be bolder and more daring at all moments in the match. On and off the pitch I walk with my head held high and shoulders back.

	Mo	Tu	Wed	Th	Fr	Sa	Su
How aware of my goal was I today?	5	4	4	3	5	1	3
How did I do with Friendly Eyes and Good Mistakes?	5	3	3	2	3	4	4
Was I aware of my trigger words?	V	V	V	X	V	V	V
Did I do the 3 minutes breathing?	V	V	V	V	V	X	V
Did I visualise how to achieve my goal for 2 minutes?	V	V	V	V	V	X	V
Did I get feedback from my buddy?	-	-	-	-	V	-	-

When did I best apply Friendly Eyes and Good Mistakes this week?
In the match on Saturday, I got frustrated because everybody could see that my long precision pass wasn't going well. But then in the practice match on Monday, for the first time ever, I managed to keep calm and instead of avoiding making those passes, I was daring. I kept repeating 'Friendly Eyes and Good mistakes' to myself and this helped.
What moment this week can I learn the most from?
Though I didn't manage to be daring during the match on Saturday and started tensing up. I also forgot to be bold and daring and didn't check that my head and shoulders were uprightor breath deeply 3 times. Good thing is, I changed this on Monday and I didn't punish myselfafter the match like I normally do. Next time I will remember!
What went well with how I communicated with myself and others this week?
In spite of the fact that there wasn't much difference in me being bolder and more daring in the match. I didn't become despondent. I was kind to myself and saw some improvement, that gives me the energy to keep going. Also I really enjoyed talking with my buddy about my Mindset goal. She/he said that there was a clear improvement in how I walked tall in the practice match, that was great to hear.

CHOOSE YOUR MINDSET GOAL NOW

Lay this book next to your bed so that it is easy to remember to fill it in. Review points 1 and 3 every morning before you do your breathing and visualisation, so that you remain committed and concentrated on what you want to achieve. Score yourself every evening from 1 to 5 (1 = unaware 5 = highly aware). Do not get down on yourself if you are often unaware. This will change with time.

1. Mindset goal - what do I want to achieve?

____

____

____

____

2. What is holding me back?

____

____

____

____

3. What do I stand to gain if I work on my chosen goal?

____

____

____

____

4. How am I going to achieve this?

a) Apply Friendly Eyes and Good Mistakes throughout the day.

b) My trigger word(s) are ______________________________

I put them on my ______________________________

c) I lower and deepen my breath every morning for 3 minutes before I visualise.

d) I visualise every morning for 2 minutes what I will do differently to achieve my goal.

e) Every evening, after reflecting on my *Mindset* goal, I fill in my success plan.

5. My buddy is... and I get feedback every week on...

6. My six week period is from: ___/___/20__ until ___/___/20__

NAME ______________________________

WHAT DO I WANT? ______________________________

	Mo	Tu	Wed	Th	Fr	Sa	Su
How aware of my goal was I today?							
How did I do with Friendly Eyes and Good Mistakes?							
Was I aware of my trigger words?							
Did I do the 3 minutes breathing?							
Did I visualise how to achieve my goal for 2 minutes?							
Did I get feedback from my buddy?							

When did I best apply Friendly Eyes and Good Mistakes this week?

What moment this week can I learn the most from about my *Mindset* goal?

What went well with how I communicated with myself and others this week?

NAME ______________________________

WHAT DO I WANT? ______________________________

	Mo	Tu	Wed	Th	Fr	Sa	Su
How aware of my goal was I today?							
How did I do with Friendly Eyes and Good Mistakes?							
Was I aware of my trigger words?							
Did I do the 3 minutes breathing?							
Did I visualise how to achieve my goal for 2 minutes?							
Did I get feedback from my buddy?							

When did I best apply Friendly Eyes and Good Mistakes this week?

____

____

____

____

What moment this week can I learn the most from about my *Mindset* goal?

____

____

____

____

What went well with how I communicated with myself and others this week?

____

____

____

____

____

NAME ______________________________

WHAT DO I WANT? ______________________________

	Mo	Tu	Wed	Th	Fr	Sa	Su
How aware of my goal was I today?							
How did I do with Friendly Eyes and Good Mistakes?							
Was I aware of my trigger words?							
Did I do the 3 minutes breathing?							
Did I visualise how to achieve my goal for 2 minutes?							
Did I get feedback from my buddy?							

When did I best apply Friendly Eyes and Good Mistakes this week?

What moment this week can I learn the most from about my *Mindset* goal?

What went well with how I communicated with myself and others this week?

NAME ____

WHAT DO I WANT? ______________________________________

	Mo	Tu	Wed	Th	Fr	Sa	Su
How aware of my goal was I today?							
How did I do with Friendly Eyes and Good Mistakes?							
Was I aware of my trigger words?							
Did I do the 3 minutes breathing?							
Did I visualise how to achieve my goal for 2 minutes?							
Did I get feedback from my buddy?							

When did I best apply Friendly Eyes and Good Mistakes this week?

____

____

____

____

What moment this week can I learn the most from about my *Mindset* goal?

____

____

____

____

What went well with how I communicated with myself and others this week?

____

____

____

____

____

NAME ____________________

WHAT DO I WANT? ____________________

	Mo	Tu	Wed	Th	Fr	Sa	Su
How aware of my goal was I today?							
How did I do with Friendly Eyes and Good Mistakes?							
Was I aware of my trigger words?							
Did I do the 3 minutes breathing?							
Did I visualise how to achieve my goal for 2 minutes?							
Did I get feedback from my buddy?							

When did I best apply Friendly Eyes and Good Mistakes this week?

What moment this week can I learn the most from about my *Mindset* goal?

What went well with how I communicated with myself and others this week?

NAME ____

WHAT DO I WANT? ____________________________________

	Mo	Tu	Wed	Th	Fr	Sa	Su
How aware of my goal was I today?							
How did I do with Friendly Eyes and Good Mistakes?							
Was I aware of my trigger words?							
Did I do the 3 minutes breathing?							
Did I visualise how to achieve my goal for 2 minutes?							
Did I get feedback from my buddy?							

When did I best apply Friendly Eyes and Good Mistakes this week?

____

____

____

____

What moment this week can I learn the most from about my *Mindset* goal?

____

____

____

____

What went well with how I communicated with myself and others this week?

____

____

____

____

____

EVALUATING YOUR MINDSET GOAL

You now know which practical Instruments you can use to deal with nerves, anger and frustration. You surely recognise moments when you lack concentration more quickly. Becoming aware of Friendly Eyes and Good Mistakes will have helped you when emotions presented themselves that might get in the way of you achieving your goal. When you reflect on this it is important to acknowledge that you have made enormous progression! It may be that you pick up on your emotions too late and they still have a hold on you or that your concentration still slips away occasionally. Realise that this is not bad at all. The greatest victory is knowing that you can do something about it and knowing what to do.

RECOGNISING WHAT YOU HAVE ACCOMPLISHED

I can say with certainty to anyone who has exercised daily for six weeks that you are mentally further along the path now than you were six weeks ago. How can I be so sure? Look back at your notes, be observant, see how your mindset has moved forward regarding your chosen goal. Let everything you have written and experienced about achieving your goal come back to you. Be happy and satisfied with yourself, even if the progress you made is modest. It's not about huge victories that can be achieved in one fell swoop. What matters most is that you experience the beginning of an awareness process and realise that by being consistent in what you want to achieve you will be able to bring about change. Through the ups and downs during the six weeks it becomes much clearer why applying Friendly Eyes and Good Mistakes is so important. It always gives you the energy to start again.

INSIGHTS

Mental progress is a path, which we walk for a lifetime and it never ends. Thank goodness because managing yourself from kindness and approaching others in this way not only improves your game, but also ensures that we live in a better world!

Please read 'a story to end with' on page 219. It will give you even more insights into why it is so worthwhile to keep taking on every challenge that arises with enjoyment, enthusiasm or acceptance and constantly stay on the path of inner growth.

EXAMPLE: STICKING TO MY TASK

What do I want to achieve?

Having total clarity of what my task is and focusing specifically on that only. Constantly being focused on what matters. No longer letting myself be influenced by outside influences such as the behaviour of our opponents, the opposing coach or the spectators from the other team.

What is holding me back?

I always see everything around me! My coach, the spectators, I am quickly impressed by our opponents (their speed, skills, outfits), and their big mouths and comments. I never just keep myself to the game, am always busy with others.

What do I stand to gain, on and off the field?

I would perform with a totally different feeling, as a much better and stronger person and a better and stronger athlete. I think it would be wonderful to feel completely 'in charge' without being influenced. No doubt, this will have a positive impact on my level of play and my team-mates. This will improve the results in the long run.

How am I going to achieve this?

a. Apply Friendly Eyes and Good Mistakes when I notice that I've lost focus of my task.
b. My trigger words are: focus on your task
c. I lower and deepen my breath every morning for 3 minutes before I visualise.
d. I visualise exactly what I am doing with my eyes, what I am paying attention to, what I am reacting to and not reacting to. I see myself at half-time reading the trigger words, 'focus on your task. I see what effect it has on me during the game. When an opponent shouts something at me, I don't react and keep my eyes where they need to be.

EXAMPLE: CONCENTRATION

What do I want to achieve?

I want to keep my concentration for longer so that I perform to the best of my ability on and off the football pitch. Especially in matches, I want to stay focused until the last second.

What is holding me back?

I am too easily distracted. Preoccupy myself with too many things. I see everything around me and cannot close myself off from it. As a result, I don't anticipate properly and make the wrong tactical decisions. I also notice that I am constantly thinking and literally forget to scan and zoom.

What do I stand to gain, on and off the field?

Much better anticipation and understanding of the game. My tactical choices will be better and my positioning will improve. Because of this change, I will be more motivated in training and playing matches will be more fun. This will mean better results for me and the team.

How am I going to achieve this?

I will revisit the assignments in Chapter 5 to gain insight into what exactly is distracting me and remind myself how to practise concentration practically.

a. I will use Friendly Eyes and Good Mistakes when I notice I am not paying attention.
b. My trigger words are scan and zoom / FOCUS.
c. I lower and deepen my breath every morning for 3 minutes before I visualise.
d. I visualise how I use eye control at the moments when the ball is out of play, so that I'm not distracted by all kinds of other things. I train myself to zoom in on my left football boot first and then scan the pitch to see where I can best take position. I continue to do this until just before play resumes. I know it will help me stay present and concentrated. When in training, I see the ball when it touches my foot and also listen to the sound of the ball against my boot. This is an excellent practice zooming and focus. I enjoy how this increases my concentration immensely.

EXAMPLE: PATIENCE

What do I want to achieve?

To be more patient and calmer in matches, especially when we haven't scored.

What is holding me back?

When it takes too long to score a goal, I get impatient. I want us to score in the first half and get irritated if we don't succeed. When we miss chances, I get angry. I start rushing more and more. Especially when the opposing team scores first, that is the worst.

What do I stand to gain, on and off the field?

By being patient, I will make better decisions and thus suffer less ball loss. By making the right choices at the right moments, my self-confidence will grow. It will feel different, I'll have more time and energy. This will improve my self-respect and my teammates and coach will respect me more.

How am I going to achieve this?

a. I will use Friendly Eyes and Good Mistakes when I notice I am starting to get impatient.
b. My trigger words are: patience / persistence
c. I lower and deepen my breath every morning for 3 minutes before I visualise.
d. I visualise how I consciously take more time during moments that I can catch my breath. And at half-time I make sure that I am calmer by lowering my breathe. This prevents me from starting the second half in a rush, especially when it is 0-0. I see myself consistently using rituals when the ball is momentarily out of play to get myself away from hurried behaviour and bring patience back into my approach.

EXAMPLE: CURIOSITY (PILLAR 3)

What do I want to achieve?

To become more open and show more curiosity to my teammates and the coach. To be receptive to information provided by others around me whom I regard as 'experts' and whom I trust. To be willing to listen to other people's opinions.

What is holding me back?

I know exactly what I'm doing, I'm sure that my solutions are the best and I'm afraid that if I allow others to influence me too much, my game will suffer as a result. Plus I have to admit I don't much like hearing about the areas in which I am 'unconsciously incompetent', I find it too painful. And to tell the truth, I can be a bit stubborn.

What do I stand to gain if I work on my chosen goal?

It's possible that things that have never occurred to me might turn out to be really good ideas. I do realise, somewhere, that I would make more rapid progress if I could adopt a more open and flexible attitude. My coach and teammates would probably find me more pleasant if I were to take an interest in their opinion and I would feel less isolated. This would improve our cooperation and in the long-term help to raise the level of my game.

How am I going to achieve this?

a. Apply Friendly Eyes and Good Mistakes if I forget to ask open questions and do not listen actively.
b. My trigger words are 'open questions and active listening'.
c. I lower my breath every morning for 3 minutes before I visualise.
d. I visualise every morning for 2 minutes a situation where I would normally close myself off and not listen actively. I see myself changing this and prepare an open question so that when the situation might occur I will know how to deal with it and what to ask. By doing this my relationship with people around me will change and I will gain their trust. They will also feel heard as I will listen actively to their opinion. Also, the knowledge they share with me will give me more opportunities to improve my game and mentality.

EXAMPLE: REALISTIC GOALS (PILLAR 4 SELF-KNOWLEDGE)

What do I want to achieve?
To learn how to choose realistic goals. Sometimes I think I can vastly improve my game within a week! I know this is not achievable and yet I can't help wanting it. During matches I think: 'oh, if someone would just give me the right tip, I could score in no time!'

What is holding me back?
I can't stand the fact that I haven't mastered the game to perfection yet. When I think about this more deeply, I realise that my emotions are totally taking control of me. Of course, it is ludicrous that I think like this and can get everything done right away. It is time I started to see the humour in this. This will make it easier to set new achievable goals.

What do I stand to gain, on and off the field?
My frustration of not being able to execute a pass will disappear. I will play with what is in my suitcase. During games, I will not crave magical solutions but just focus on working hard. This will bring mental peace and steady progress will be within reach. As a result, I will play with more confidence and I know my coach and teammates will be happy to help me with this. Together we will become stronger.

How am I going to achieve this?
a. I will use Friendly Eyes and Good Mistakes when I notice that my goals are unrealistic, smile and continue with my focus on an achievable goal.
b. My trigger words are: be realistic / smile.
c. I lower and deepen my breath every morning for 3 minutes before I visualise.
d. I visualise being fully present during the match. I see myself checking with the coach before training sessions and matches that my goal is realistic. My attention is on what is achievable and what we've agreed to. I see possibilities and that is enough and gives me confidence. I feel it. Win or lose, I see myself enjoying the game at my current level.

EXAMPLE: SELF-DISCPLINE GOALS (PILLAR 5)

What do I want to achieve?

I really want to keep to the promises I make with myself, my teammates and my coach. When I say I want to achieve a certain goal, I want to do everything within my power to improve that aspect of my game. I will push forward.

What is holding me back?

I have so often set goals in my life that didn't work out, so I now have little belief or confidence in my ability to change this. I have lost the enthusiasm to persevere. To be honest: it's much easier to give up. I usually do, I'm used to that, and with me many other players. As a result, I don't feel so annoyed by it.

What do I stand to gain, on and off the field?

When I train and play with self-discipline every time, I know I will feel much better. It will help me boost my self-confidence and no doubt it will benefit my game. My coach and teammates will be happy that they no longer have to motivate and encourage me the whole time. The bond with them will be much better because I am 100 per cent committed. I hopefully I'll inspire some of the others to also start giving their best in every training and match.

How am I going to achieve this?

a. I will use Friendly Eyes and Good Mistakes when I notice my old patterns
b. My trigger words are: step by step, climb the mountain
c. I lower and deepen my breath every morning for 3 minutes before I visualise.
d. I visualise every morning that I persevere until the end of each exercise and thus the whole training. I see myself getting tired, then instead of giving up, I focus my attention on my breathing and trigger words, which keep me going. I see myself being successful in completing the schedule every night and how happy that makes me. I see myself playing a match from the first to the last minute with true effort. It makes me feel proud.

EXAMPLE: ACCEPTANCE (PILLAR 6)

What do I want to achieve?

I would like to learn to accept what is inevitable and not get so upset about it. I will then be able to use energy much better for things that matter and that I can influence. I want to learn how to not be constantly overwhelmed by emotions. Especially at moments when I think my opponent is trying to annoy me.

What is holding me back?

I know it's pointless, but it seems like I enjoy cultivating not being satisfied with things, being irritated and allowing myself to linger on those emotions. I often feel like 'things happen to me'. It's something I don't believe I can get under control.

What do I stand to gain, on and off the field?

Through acceptance, I would be able to transform the senseless loss of energy into powerful positive action and growth. Acceptance helps me to feel calm and free and get over my irritations. This allows me to refocus my attention on the game. My concentration will improve and I will achieve more. I will become much more balanced.

How am I going to achieve this?

a. Friendly Eyes and Good Mistakes will help me notice that earlier when I am stuck in my emotions. I am happy to recognise and admit this.
b. My trigger word is: Acceptance
c. I lower and deepen my breath every morning for 3 minutes before I visualise.
d. I visualise every morning focusing my attention on my breathing instead of being preoccupied with the opponent's behaviour. This will keep me to be calmer and more focused. I see all of the situations that would normally get me really angry, and see that it is possible to do things differently and what an amazing effect that will have on the team. It will also stop anybody or anything having control over me. I will master myself and learn to accept things.

EXAMPLE: PERSEVERANCE

What do I want?

Fight to the end. Radiate and feel that I never give up. Walk with my head held high regardless of the score.

What is holding me back?

I consider myself a loser. When the going gets tough, I just seem to lose the way and am clueless what to do. I become convinced that there is no point in trying my best anymore, I've never been able to find that inner strength and it just doesn't work like that for me until now. I can no longer muster the energy to be physically present.

What do I stand to gain, on and off the field?

Everything will change if I can persevere to the end. I will have more self-respect, get a better relationship with my teammates and my coach. Instead of feeling like a loser, I will feel good about giving my all. In the long run, this will also improve results. I will feel satisfied with myself and this is a feeling I really want, instead of constant disappointment.

How am I going to achieve this?

a. Use Friendly Eyes and Good Mistakes even when it feels weird if I'm feeling down.
b. My trigger words are: keep going, you've got this, walk tall!
c. I lower and deepen my breath every morning for 3 minutes before I visualise.
d. I visualise myself singing Rocky's song 'The Eye of the Tiger' to get myself into the right 'feeling'. I see myself standing on the pitch, shaking my muscles completely loose to make sure I am physically present and playing at a constant 'alert' tempo. Regardless of the score, I walk upright at a brisk pace throughout the match, radiating energy.

A STORY TO END WITH

STRUGGLE

Once upon a time, there was a celebrated athlete who lived in a remote kingdom. He never had to make the slightest effort. He did not have to train for hours to strengthen his body and his mind. He did not have to repeat the same monotonous exercises every day. He did not have to slave away at improving his skills, since they had been perfect from the outset.

In matches, his supremacy was so awesome that his opponents never got under his skin or needled him, or roused him to greater achievements. But since he always won with ease, he never experienced the pleasure of a duel or a hard-fought victory, the pleasure of coming from behind to win, or the joy of physical and mental satisfaction after a struggle.

– Bob Mitchell: *The Tao of Sport*

ACKNOWLEDGEMENTS

First and foremost, we would like to thank our partners Jacqueline van Meyel and Stasja Draisma, who have been with us since the very start of the *Mindset* Expedition in 2007. Without them there would be no *Mindset*.

It is an honour to dedicate this book to former Dutch International, Willy Dullens, one of the most talented players in the history of Dutch football. He got tragically injured at the young age of 21. After multiple operations his knee never fully recovered. Johan Cruyff said of Willy that 'he was technically a better player than I was.'

We are deeply honoured that Sarina Wiegman recognises our work and is a Friendly Eyes ambassador. Sarina's substantial help with a number of the football examples in this book shows her commitment to detail, her dedication and expertise and how generous she is with her time and knowledge. Thank you Sarina.

Evelyne Dullens, ex-tennis international and Jackie's assistant with Friendly Eyes since 2008, has been an unmissable force. Evelyne is Willy's daughter, hence the surname! We are deeply grateful to both of them for their support with the content for the football examples. Evelyne has also played an important role in the filming of the online courses.

Many thanks to the 10-year football collaboration that Jackie enjoyed with Maria van Kortenhof and Hesterine de Reus from 2008 to 2018. Both coaches are pioneers in women's football and we are grateful to them for their lifetime commitment to the game.

Roos Kwakkenbos has been a great help to us. We needed someone who understood English football terminology. Roos fulfilled that role perfectly and with commitment and passion, translated the football examples from Dutch to English.

We were fortunate enough to find a true expert in Joanne Haslett, a professional translator and proofreader. Her understanding of the English language and enthusiasm for the content, made the last part of our work a collaborative joy.

Finally, we would like to thank our three other Friendly Eyes ambassadors who generously support the mindset revolution. Pieter van den Hoogenband, three times Olympic Champion Swimming, Chef de Mission of the Dutch Olympic Games, Barbara Hannigan, Canadian opera singer and conductor, Grammy Award winner and Sven Groeneveld, professional tennis coach, former coach of: Roger Federer, Esther Vergeer, Maria Sharapova, Bianca Andreescu, Michael Stich and many more.

There are so many other generous people who have offered their support, you know who you are, we thank you from the bottom of our hearts for helping us with the *Mindset* Revolution.

RECOMMENDED READING

Andy West: *Lionel Messi and the Art of Living*. Pitch Publishing Ltd 2018

Kobe Bryant: *The Mamba Mentality: How I Play*. MCD, 2018

Timothy Ferris: *Tools of Titans: The Tactics, Routines, and Habits of Billionaires, Icons, and World-Class Performers*. Houghton Mifflin Harcourt, 2016

Michael A. Singer: *The untethered soul*. New Harbinger Publications, 2007

Marshall B. Rosenberg: *Nonviolent communication*. Puddle Dancer Press, 2015

Melody Beattie: *Codependent No More*. Spiegel & Grau, 2022

Michael A. Singer: *The surrender experiment*. Hodder & Stoughton, 2016

Novak Djokovic: *Serve to win*. Corgi Books, 2014

Jon Kabat-Zinn: *Wherever you go, there you are*. Hachette Books

George Mumford: *The Mindful Athlete*. Parallax Press, 2015

Daniel Kahneman: *Thinking, Fast and Slow*. Penguin Books Ltd, 2012

Carol Dweck: *Mindset: The New Psychology of Success*. Random House Books. New York, U.S.A., 2006

W. Timothy Gallway: *The Inner Game of Tennis*. Random House. New York, 1974

Andy Puddicombe: *Get some Head Space*. St. Martin's Press, 175 Fifth Avenue, New York, 2011

The work of S.N. Goenka - www.dhamma.org

William Hart: *The art of living*. Harper. San Francisco, 1987

Eckhart Tolle: *The Power of Now*. New World Library. USA, 1999

Jill Bolte Taylor: *My Stroke of Insight: A Brain Scientist's Personal Journey.* Viking Penguin. U.S.A., 2008

Daniel Coyle: *The Talent Code.* Random House Books.New York, U.S.A., 2009

Stephen R. Covey: *The Seven Habits of Highly Effective People.* Simon & Schuster. New York, 1999

B.K.S. Iyengar: *Light on Yoga.* Schocken Books. New York, 1966

Dan Millman: *The Inner Athlete.* Stillpoint publishing. New Hampshire, U.S.A., 1994

John Douillard: *Body, Mind and Sport.* Three Rivers Press. New York, U.S.A., 1994

Joseph Goldstein: *Insight Meditation.* Shambhala Publications, Inc. Boston, Massachusetts, 1993

Joe Dispenza: *Breaking the habit of being yourself.* Hay House Inc. 2016

Jackie Reardon and Hans Dekkers: *Mindset: a mental guide for sport.* Mindset Publishers 2016

Jackie Reardon and Hans Dekkers: *Mindset in Daily Life: chasing the mosquitoes away.* Mindset Publishers 2013

Printed in Great Britain
by Amazon

36826445R00126